A Return to
VIRTUE

A Return to
VIRTUE

ELAINE S. DALTON

DESERET
BOOK

Salt Lake City, Utah

Library of Congress Cataloging-in-Publication Data

Dalton, Elaine S. (Elaine Schwartz), author.
    A return to virtue / Elaine S. Dalton.
        pages cm
    Includes bibliographical references and index.
    ISBN 978-1-60908-924-5 (hardbound : alk. paper)
    1. Conduct of life.   2. Christian life—Mormon authors.   3. The Church of Jesus
Christ of Latter-day Saints—Doctrines.   I. Title.
    BJ1589.D35 2011
    248.4'893—dc23   2011025985

Printed in the United States of America
Publishers Printing, Salt Lake City, UT

10   9   8   7   6   5   4   3   2

To my husband, who sets a fast pace on the right path

*To our children, who have run ahead and
motivated me to be better*

*To my mother, who trained me in
persistence and exactness*

To my father, who leads the way

To our grandchildren, who will follow in our footsteps

To Eliza, who has already crossed the finish line

CONTENTS

Contents

"There is no resting place along the path called faithfulness. The trek is constant, and no lingering is allowed."

—President Thomas S. Monson

INTRODUCTION

Shortly after our oldest son, Matt, left on his mission, I determined that I would try to develop the same discipline and self-control in my life that he was developing as a missionary. I wanted to do something hard—something that seemed impossible to me. I decided to run a marathon.

Running a marathon would require things of me that were similar to what Matt was experiencing. For one, I would have to wake up early. I would have to train whether it was hot or cold, sunny or stormy. I would have to do this daily, running the exact number of miles on the plan that mapped out how to prepare for a marathon. I also determined to read my scriptures before I ran so that I would have something to think about if I ran alone and something to share if I ran with someone else.

The plan was set. Each day when the alarm went off and I got up, I would think of my son doing the same thing—waking up to read and study the word of God and then going forth to do what he had committed to do.

After a year of preparation, when I crossed the finish line in the first marathon I had ever run, I knew something about myself I hadn't known before. I knew I could do hard things.

As I searched the scriptures on those early mornings, I discovered that others had also done hard things—much harder than what I was doing. I was tutored by their examples of diligence, prayer, and testimony. I read of Hannah, who gave her precious child to the Lord to serve Him in the temple for the rest of his life. I cried when I learned that every year she came to visit her son and brought a little coat for him. I could imagine her sewing that coat so her son would be warm and would feel her loving arms around him. I could imagine her picturing her son in her mind, thinking about how much he might have grown since the last time she saw him. Hannah did a hard thing—because she had made a covenant with the Lord and she believed His promises.

Nephi, too, did many hard things. He left his home in Jerusalem. He returned twice—to obtain the plates of Laban and to bring Ishmael's family into the wilderness. I wonder if he would have said, "It's too hard" if he had allowed himself to think too much about what his father was asking him to do. That was certainly what his brothers said. But Nephi prayed to Heavenly Father to help him know the things his father knew. He received a testimony. He believed. He knew the Lord would prepare a way for him to accomplish anything that was asked.

I find myself now with new "hard things" to accomplish, with the Lord's help. For example, I never imagined I would write a book. When I did realize that this was going to happen, I thought that, because of my responsibilities as Young Women general president, I would likely be directing the book to young women.

As it took shape, however, it became evident that the message of virtue is one for all of us, not just the next generation. And so the book is intended for a general audience, although I could not resist devoting one full chapter specifically to the young women I have grown to love so much. It's not the way I imagined it would be, but that was how it turned out.

Even further from my imagination was the thought of the topic "a return to virtue." But in my life I have somehow always known the importance of virtue. Virtue, for me, is a pattern of thought and behavior based on high moral standards. It encompasses chastity and sexual purity. These standards seem to have always been a part of me, most likely because of the home in which I was raised and the role models I had in my childhood and youth. My mother is a virtuous, incredible woman, and I owe her much of the credit for who I am today and what I value.

As for a *return* to virtue, I have always believed that returning is possible. *Returning* means coming full circle to the place where we began. Returning to the presence of our loving Heavenly Father has always been my desire. In another sense, *returning* can mean turning around, getting on the right course, or admitting a mistake. The Atonement of Jesus Christ makes it possible for those who have strayed from the path to repent and return.

Beyond this, we need to stand for virtue in a world that is so rapidly departing from it. We need to call for a return to virtue in our society at large.

Could it be that we have been slowly desensitized into thinking that high moral standards are old-fashioned and not relevant or important in today's society? We can learn a lesson from

Lehonti in the Book of Mormon, whose army was well positioned on the top of a mountain, "fixed in their minds with a determined resolution" that they would not be forced by Amalickiah to go to war against the Nephites (Alma 47:6). It took the deceitful Amalickiah only four tries, each one more bold than the previous, to get Lehonti to "come down off from the mount" (v. 12). Then, having embraced Amalickiah's false promises, Lehonti was "poison[ed] by degrees" (v. 18) until he died.

Not just poisoned, but "by degrees." Could this be happening today? Could it be that we have been decieved by false role models and persuasive media messages that cause us to forget our divine identity? Are we too being poisoned by degrees? What could be more deceptive than to entice us to do nothing or to be busy ever texting but never coming to a knowledge of the truths contained in a book that was written for our day by prophets of God: the Book of Mormon? What could be more deceptive than to entice women, young and old, you and me, to be so involved in ourselves, our looks, our clothes, our body shape and size that we lose sight of our divine identity and our ability to change the world through our virtuous influence? What could be more deceptive than to entice men, young and old, holding the priesthood of God, to view seductive pornography and thus focus on flesh instead of faith, to be consumers of vice rather than guardians of virtue?

The Book of Mormon relates the story of two thousand young heroes whose virtue and purity gave them the strength to defend their parents' covenants and their families' faith (see Alma

56–58). Their virtue and commitment to be true at all times changed the world!

And so I have embarked on a journey to reinstate the word *virtue* into our vocabulary and our lives, and to reinstate the core meaning of the word, which is purity and power. I believe that purity—yes, virtue—yields power. The power of which I speak is the power that comes of confidence, and that confidence comes as we allow virtue to be a part of our thoughts and our actions.

So how do virtue and running fit together? Again, just as I never imagined I would write a book, I also never imagined I would run a marathon, let alone seventeen of them! And as I began my first marathon, I never really thought I would live to tell about it! It seemed an impossible goal and achievement to me. But perhaps some also feel this is the case with remaining virtuous and chaste in today's world. What I have learned is that neither running a marathon nor remaining virtuous—or returning to virtue—is impossible. In fact, I believe that a return to virtue is important, even critical, for the future of our families and our communities, our country, and our civilization.

Running a marathon requires strict training. It requires self-discipline. It requires daily diligence in our habits and our actions. So does remaining virtuous and pure before marriage and true and faithful after marriage. Championing virtue requires developing holy habits and righteous routines. It requires that we come out from the world and be separate. Self-discipline, self-denial, and self-direction are essential.

A marathon closely parallels life itself. Sometimes we train alone, sometimes we train in groups. We get injured, we heal, we fall and get back up, and, yes, we take wrong turns and then we return. We have times of great triumph and times of great trial. We are required to push through the pain and keep going. We learn that we never really run alone and that there are scores of angels who guide and guard our journey. And we come, somehow, in the doing of it all, to realize that our life has purpose and that what we do or don't do matters. We also realize that we cannot counterfeit adequate training. We cannot cheat when it comes to putting in the miles it takes to be strong enough to run a marathon.

Most important, we come to know that we are not in this human race alone. We learn that how we treat and respect each other matters—that we are divine in our nature and that we are all of infinite worth. A virtuous life is a life that acknowledges this fact in us and in others.

Returning to virtue is not a solitary pursuit. In order to remain virtuous, we need each other. We will all need to help each other, and if one of us falls or fails, we can help him or her "return." We must remember that we are journeying through mortality not for our own selfish interests, but to help others be victorious as well. In 1976, at a track-and-field event in Spokane, Washington, a group of young athletes gathered at the starting line, ready to fulfill the oath they took as Special Olympians: "Let me win. But if I cannot win, let me be brave in the attempt." The gun fired, and the race began—for all but one boy, who stumbled and began to cry. Hearing his cries, one or two other runners stopped, turned around, and helped the fallen young man cross the finish line. I imagine that the cheers coming from the crowd for the actual winner of this race were just as much for the young man who fell and the champions who bravely turned around and helped their friend finish the race.

Why? Because deep down we know that what matters in this life is more than winning for ourselves. What matters is helping others win, even if it means slowing down and changing our course. Life teaches us that we can achieve happiness when we seek the happiness and well-being of others.

When I attended the blessing of one of our granddaughters, it was a holy sight to me as my husband and our sons, along with many other loved ones, encircled this little infant. She was so elegant all dressed in white—and it didn't hurt a bit that she was named after her two grandmothers! But the thing that touched me most was the blessing given by her father, our son Zach. He blessed little Annabel Elaine that she would understand her identity as a daughter of God, that she would follow the examples of her mother, grandmothers, and sister, and that she would find great joy as she lived a virtuous life and prepared to make and keep sacred temple covenants. In that moment, I prayed that every young woman might be encircled, strengthened, and protected by righteous priesthood power, not only at the time of birth and blessing but throughout life.

© bu Intellectual Reserve, Inc.

Annabel Elaine Dalton, encircled by priesthood power

Also among those who will encircle us is the Savior, who has walked the path before and marked the way. He knows how to succor us. He will pick us up, He will strengthen us, and He will help us cross the finish line and return to His presence—proven and pure.

In the final chapters of the Book of Mormon, a book written for us and our day, Moroni records his own and his father's last exhortations to each of us. Mormon reminds us of the wickedness and depravity that had destroyed an entire civilization. His eyewitness account of what happens to individuals and societies when virtue is absent motivates his final plea to us: "And again I would exhort you that ye would come unto Christ, and lay hold upon every good gift, and *touch not the evil gift, nor the unclean thing*" (Moroni 10:30; emphasis added).

Why a return to virtue? Why a marathon analogy? Why now? Why me? Perhaps it is because I have learned that the marathon of life will require all that we have. It will require strict training. It will require that we help others along our path. It will require strength beyond our own, and this will require purity and virtue. And mostly I know through personal experience that each of our divine missions depends on the strength that can be derived only by patterning our lives after the Savior. He is our exemplar, He is our enabler, He is our Redeemer. This is our goal, this is our aim, and this is the quest of a lifetime: "That when he shall appear we shall be like him, for we shall see him as he is; that we may have this hope; that we may be purified even as he is pure" (Moroni 7:48).

Juma Ikangaa, the Tanzanian runner and winner of multiple marathons, including the New York Marathon, often said something I will never forget: "The will to win means nothing without the will to prepare" (Sandrock, "Juma Ikangaa," in *Running with Legends*, 415). It is my hope that this book will help all of us prepare to run well the race that is set before us.

Chapter 1

ORIENTATION

Welcome to the Race

Several years ago, I qualified to run the Boston Marathon. The night before the marathon, in an effort to visualize what it would be like to complete the race, my husband and I went to downtown Boston, about a mile from the finish line. There, in the quiet of the evening, we laced up our running shoes and ran that last mile to the finish. As we crossed the line, we held our hands victoriously high in the air and pretended that we had won the race! We imagined thousands of observers in the stands cheering for us.

The next day, we ran the actual race. Twenty-six point two miles (41.3 km) is a challenging distance. There are hills called "Heartbreak" for a very good reason. The entire time I ran those hills, I kept in mind the finish line and what it had felt like the night before to cross it victorious. That vision helped me to finish the marathon in a pelting, cold, New England storm.

Our vision of the future will help us press forward. As we prepare to succeed in this marathon of mortal life, we might like to start by taking a few minutes to envision where we want to be in one year or two or five. Then we need to take action to prepare ourselves. People don't just run a marathon when they decide to do it. They must train daily, slowly building stamina and endurance to run the 26.2-mile distance. So it is with life. It is daily diligence with prayer and scripture study that will help us reach our goals. Our daily decisions will influence not only our own present and future lives but the lives of generations to come.

STRICT TRAINING

Each one of us has embarked on a journey as a Latter-day Saint. Successful completion of our journey will require strict training. There is no better time than now for us to form eternal habits and make lasting decisions. We have been reserved "for such a time as this" (Esther 4:14). We will be presented with opportunities that far surpass our greatest expectations. Ours is the challenge and blessing to lead the world in a return to virtue.

What is virtue? Why is it important? And how can each of us join together in this noble and sacred cause?

Let me begin with a simple story of a nine-year-old pioneer girl named Agnes Caldwell. Of her experience in the Willie Handcart Company in 1856, Agnes related: "Although only tender years of age, I can yet close my eyes and see everything in panoramic precision before me—the ceaseless walking, walking, ever to remain in my memory. Many times I would become so tired and, childlike, would hang on the cart, only to be gently pushed away. Then I would throw myself by the side of the road and cry. Then realizing they were all passing me by, I would jump to my feet and make an extra run to catch up."

She goes on to share: "Just before we crossed the mountains, relief wagons reached us, and it certainly was a relief. The infirm and aged were allowed to ride, all able-bodied continuing to walk. When the wagons started out, a number of us children decided to see how long we could keep up with the wagons, in hopes of being asked to ride. At least that is what my great hope was. One by one they all fell out, until I was the last one remaining, so determined was I that I should get a ride. After what seemed the longest run I ever made before or since, the driver . . . called to me, 'Say, sissy, would you like a ride?' I answered in my very best manner, 'Yes sir.' At this he reached over, taking my hand, clucking to his horses to make me run, with legs that seemed to me could run no farther. On we went, to what to me seemed miles. What went through my head at that time was that he was the meanest man that ever lived. . . . Just at what seemed the breaking point, he stopped. Taking a blanket, he wrapped me up and lay me in the bottom of the wagon, warm and comfortable. Here I had time to change my mind, as I surely did, knowing full well by doing this he saved me from freezing when taken into the wagon" (in Madsen, *I Walked to Zion*, 57–59).

Young Agnes Caldwell made it safely to the Salt Lake Valley in November 1856. Her family settled in Brigham City, Utah, where Agnes met and married Chester Southworth. Together, they had thirteen children and, among other righteous service in the kingdom, helped settle a Latter-day Saint colony in Cardston, Alberta, Canada.

Had the driver of that wagon taken Agnes into the wagon without making her run, she would have surely succumbed to the bitter cold. And had Agnes chosen to give up and fall behind, her story may have ended much differently. However, for Agnes this became her defining moment, and though the decision to run did not make perfect sense at the time, she ran anyway. She ran toward Zion—following in the footsteps of the prophet Brigham Young and heeding the voice of the Lord, who said, "Let them awake, and arise, and come forth, and not tarry, for I, the Lord, command it" (Doctrine and Covenants 117:2).

This was the run of her life! It was hard, and she resisted. But by running she was able to generate enough body heat to keep warm and prevent her from freezing during her ride in the wagon.

Each of us is on a journey to Zion, and, like Agnes did, we too must "Awake, and arise, and come forth, and not tarry" (Doctrine and Covenants 117:2). We must remember that Zion is not only a place, it is a state of being, it is "the pure in heart" (Doctrine and Covenants 97:21). And purity of heart must be our goal in order to reach our final destination. We are better pre-pared and better equipped than any people in the history of the world. We have what it takes, and now is the time for the run of our lives—our run to Zion!

President Thomas S. Monson and those before him have shown us the way. The course is clearly marked, and the pace is steady and strong. We, like Agnes, are being asked to cross the plains. We may not have to give up all of our earthly possessions, but the journey to Zion requires that we give up all of our sins so that we may come to know Him—the true and living Christ. We may even be asked to run to the point of exhaustion; but by

doing so the warmth of the Lord's love will preserve us for the great work yet to come.

In 1838, the Lord told His Saints gathered in Far West, Missouri, "Arise and shine forth, that thy light may be a standard for the nations" (Doctrine and Covenants 115:5). The pioneers, like young Agnes and her family, who faithfully endured the persecutions heaped on the early Church and then willingly walked away—to Zion—set forth a standard for the nations and for this generation. Their journey had everything to do with their faith and testimony. It had everything to do with Joseph Smith and Moroni and Oliver Cowdery and Nephi and Moses and Joshua and even Thomas S. Monson. And it had and has everything to do with you and me. They sacrificed their all in order to come to Zion and there build a temple to our God. They knew that Joseph Smith was a prophet of God and that the Book of Mormon was true. They knew that the blessings to be bestowed in holy temples were necessary for the plan to be accomplished. And they knew, as Moroni repeatedly taught Joseph Smith, that "if it were not so, the whole earth would be utterly wasted at his coming" (Joseph Smith—History 1:39).

Zion—the pure in heart—was then and is now the goal. It is the cause of the restored gospel of Jesus Christ. And now is the time, as Mormon and Moroni exhorted, to "be faithful in Christ" (Moroni 9:25) and to "lay hold upon every good gift, and touch not the evil gift, nor the unclean thing" (Moroni 10:30). Now is the time to "awake, and arise from the dust, . . . that the covenants of the Eternal Father which he hath made unto thee, O

house of Israel, may be fulfilled" (Moroni 10:31). Now is the time
to return to virtue!

A Return to Virtue Is a Return to Purity

Virtue means purity. It begins in the heart and in the mind.
"It is a pattern of thought and behavior based on high moral standards" (*Preach My Gospel,* 118). A core element of virtue, one that
is often ignored by the world, is chastity—meaning sexual purity.
Virtue and chastity are inseparably connected. You cannot have
one without the other. A return to virtue is a return to purity.
Some have said that being virtuous means being kind or honest
or having integrity—and those are important. But the center of
a virtuous life is chastity, and one simply cannot be honest or
possess integrity in the absence of sexual purity. It is impossible.
One cannot tamper with the divine spirit and precious body—the
eternal soul—of another and be deemed as possessing any kind of
virtue or be virtuous. To do this compromises the very agency we
fought for in our premortal life.

Some have suggested that virtue is primarily for women,
but it is not gender based. The Latin root word for *virtue* is *vir-
tus,* which means "strength." One contemporary meaning states
that virtue is an "effective power or force; efficacy; [especially]
the ability to heal or strengthen" (*Webster's New World College
Dictionary,* s.v. "virtue"). Thus virtue applies not just to women
but to all.

When the woman in the streets of Jerusalem reached out and
touched the hem of the Savior's garment, she knew she would be

6

healed. Why? Because she recognized His purity and His power. The Savior Himself said, "I perceive that *virtue* is gone out of me" (Luke 8:46; italics added; see also Mark 5:30; Luke 6:19). The kind of virtue to which He was referring is power, priesthood power, which always accompanies Latter-day Saint men who are pure and practice "virtue and holiness before [the Lord]" (Doctrine and Covenants 38:24).

One cold April day after general conference, I climbed Ensign Peak with my two counselors in the general Young Women presidency, Mary Cook and Ann Dibb. There we unfurled a gold Peruvian shawl—a banner calling for a return to virtue. Atop that peak, as we looked into the valley and viewed the majestic Salt Lake Temple, we knew that a return to virtue meant a return to moral purity. Virtue is the golden key that unlocks temple doors. As Elder Russell M. Nelson taught, the temple is really the reason for everything we do in the Church: "Every activity, every lesson, all we do in the Church, point to the Lord and His holy house" ("Personal Preparation for Temple Blessings," 32). Brigham Young knew that; and there atop Ensign Peak we also knew that to be true.

As we unfurled this banner to the world, we knew that a return to virtue is not only essential, it is critical. We must be worthy to enter the Lord's holy temple and make and keep sacred covenants and do the work we have been prepared and foreordained to do. No unclean thing can enter into His house.

Just as the driver of that rescue wagon saved Agnes Caldwell from freezing to death, we too have been given the opportunity and privilege to become saviors on Mount Zion—to do for others something they cannot do for themselves. This can happen only when we are worthy to make and keep sacred covenants and receive the ordinances of the temple.

Each of us has a great work to do. What you do and what you decide matters because *you* matter! You are one of the "choice spirits who were reserved to come forth in the fulness of times to take part in laying the foundations of the great latter-day work, including the building of the temples and the performance of ordinances therein" (Doctrine and Covenants 138:53–54).

No wonder Satan has increased the intensity of his attacks. If we can be distracted, delayed, or disqualified from entering into the temple and doing the very work we have been prepared and reserved to do, he wins. What becomes clear is that we must be pure and worthy in order to receive the promptings from the Holy Ghost that we need for the decisions we are making every day. What also becomes clear is that we must remain worthy to enter the Lord's holy temples.

Much of the sacrifice and work of prior generations has led to this moment. Pioneers sacrificed everything, even their lives, in order that we might see this day. Our advent on the earth is not random. This was all part of the plan we embraced in the premortal realm. We are positioned in a remarkable place in the history of the world. Never before has so much been expected. Never before has so much been given: prophets, scriptures, priesthood, ordinances and covenants, temples, the Book of Mormon, and the gospel in its fullness. We have been prepared, called, and chosen. This is our race.

To accomplish the tasks we have been foreordained to do,

our faith must be firmly centered on our Savior, Jesus Christ. We must remember that faith is a principle not only of power but of action. We must act on the faith we already possess. In the premortal realms, each one of us exhibited not just faith but "exceeding faith and good works" (Alma 13:3). As Alma said, each of us was "called and prepared from the foundation of the world according to the foreknowledge of God" (Alma 13:3). Men were prepared to receive the priesthood, which would enable them to exercise the power of God while here on the earth. Women were given the noble gift and responsibility to nurture others and become mothers to other choice spirits. We were entrusted with the very powers of godliness—to create a mortal life.

Virtuous people are committed to the sanctity of life. They respect God's counsel on how life is to be conceived, protected, and nurtured. There is no strength that is greater than the strength of virtue, nor any confidence that is more sure than the confidence of a virtuous life.

In the premortal realm we participated in a war. We fought, armed with our faith and testimonies, to accept and sustain the plan that was presented by God the Father. We knew it was right, and we knew that the Savior would do what He said He would do because we knew Him! There were no neutral spirits in the War in Heaven, and there can be no neutral positions now where choices between right and wrong are to be made. The Lord Himself said, "He that is not with me is against me" (Matthew 12:30). We stood with Him! We were eager for our mortal assignments. We knew what was going to be required of us. We knew how difficult it would be, and yet we were confident not only that we could

accomplish our divine missions but that we could make a difference. As one prophet, President Ezra Taft Benson, said of our day:

"For nearly six thousand years, God has held you in reserve
to make your appearance in the final days before the Second
Coming of the Lord. . . . God has saved for the final inning some
of his strongest children, who will help bear off the Kingdom
triumphantly. And that is where you come in, for you are the
generation that must be prepared to meet your God.

"All through the ages the prophets have looked down through
the corridors of time to our day. Billions of the deceased and
those yet to be born have their eyes on us. Make no mistake about
it—you are a marked generation" ("In His Steps," 59).

A Return to Virtue Could Save a Nation

When Peter wrote his epistle to the early Saints, he told them
to "add to [their] faith virtue" (2 Peter 1:5). Faith without virtue
would soon languish and die because without virtue there is no
purity. Without virtue there is no strength. And without virtue
there is no spirituality. It is clear that once we really understand
who we are, we must be pure because purity precedes spiritual
power (see Ballard, "Purity Precedes Power"). This is not the kind
of power we see in the world. It has nothing to do with fame,
position, good looks, celebrity, or wealth. Spiritual power and
strength have everything to do with virtue.

We live in a world that is concerned about cleanliness and purity—the cleanliness of our air and the cleanliness of our environ-
ment, our water, and even our food. In some places we legislate

against pollution and even have government-funded environmental protection agencies to ensure that we are not made ill by contaminants that get into our air, our water, or our food supply. Yet society tolerates moral pollution in the form of pornography on billboards, television, and the Internet, and in entertainment and other media. We tolerate filth that invades our minds through suggestive lyrics, music, and language. In some respects we are an organic generation, ensuring purity and quality of many things in our lives; and yet we remain oblivious to the truth that we are polluting our moral fiber. I believe that the lack of virtue in our society is directly responsible for many of our social, financial, and governmental ills. I believe that the disintegration of faith and families, and even financial unrest, are directly related to a lack of virtue in our society. And I believe that a return to virtue could save an entire nation.

We call for a social reform, but what is really needed is a moral reform—a call for a return to virtue. And if we who have been given so much, including the restored gospel of Jesus Christ, don't lead the world in that return to virtue, who will? We were leaders in the premortal world and stood for everything that is now threatened in society.

During the critical days of World War II, Winston Churchill aroused an entire nation when he said: "You ask, what is our aim? I can answer in one word: It is victory, victory at all costs, victory in spite of all terror, victory, however long and hard the road may be; for without victory, there is no survival" (in Lukas, *Blood, Toil, Tears, and Sweat*, 44). I echo that call for the war in which we are engaged today by paraphrasing the words of Winston Churchill:

You ask, what is our aim? I can answer with one word: virtue. Virtue at all costs, virtue in spite of all opposition, virtue, however long and hard the road to repentance may be; for without virtue, there can be no victory.

In the Book of Mormon, Helaman and his stripling warriors were known for their virtue and their ability to trust in their mothers' testimonies. They were "true at all times in whatsoever thing they were entrusted" (Alma 53:20). They were covenant keepers, and they fought to ensure that their parents could also keep their covenants. Victory was their aim, and virtue was their strength.

Mormon wrote to his son Moroni about the degenerate society in which he lived. He reported that the people had become so base and immoral that they didn't value those things that were "most dear and precious above all things, which is chastity and virtue" (Moroni 9:9). Could it be that we have reached this point in our society? In a bygone era, those who violated the law of chastity were branded with a scarlet letter. Now that brand and letter seems to be worn by the chaste.

We are preparing for the Savior's return. We must abhor sin. We must position and prepare ourselves now to be "more fit for the kingdom" (*Hymns,* no. 131). It has been prophesied that in a coming day, people of all nations will say, "Come ye, and let us go up to the mountain of the Lord, . . . and he will teach us of his ways, and we will walk in his paths; for out of Zion shall go forth the law" (2 Nephi 12:3). Will we be the ones to lead this ascent?

Several years ago I was running early in the morning on the day before Thanksgiving with a group of women. We called it our

Thanksgiving run, and as we ran we called out things for which we were thankful. I had just finished saying that I was thankful for a strong, healthy body when I slipped and fell on a patch of black ice on the road. As I tried to get up, I realized that I was badly hurt. I knew I had broken my leg just above the ankle—and just thinking about how I knew makes me feel a little faint. My husband said that if I had been an NFL football player, I would have made the highlight films that night.

As I lay there in the road in the shadows of the early morning light, waiting for help to arrive, I saw the lights of a car come speeding down the road right toward where I lay. The car screeched to a stop, and a man jumped out. He said he had thought I was a garbage bag in the road and almost kept going. I asked if he were a member of the Church, and he replied that he was. I asked if he could give me a blessing because the pain was so severe I didn't know how long I could stay in that condition. He paused and then said: "I can't. You better wait for your husband to do that." Then he got in his car and drove away.

When I arrived at the hospital, I was wheeled into a little cubicle in the emergency room, where I waited to be taken into surgery. As they moved the curtains to the side, there were my husband and all five of our sons. As they encircled me and laid their hands on my head, I felt their purity, their power, and their strength. I was then and am still so grateful for righteous priesthood holders who keep themselves pure so that they can be able to use their priesthood power at a moment's notice. That day I was blessed by such priesthood power, which they exercised in virtue and holiness.

REMAIN VIRTUOUS IN A TOXIC WORLD

I truly believe that one virtuous woman or man, led by the Spirit, can change the world! But before we can change the world, we must change ourselves. So what are some of the things we can do right now in order to remain virtuous in a toxic world? What are some of the miles we must run in our race to mortal victory?

First, repent. I am very aware that there are Latter-day Saints who don't feel virtuous or who have made mistakes. That is why a *return* to virtue is so important. We *can* return. We *can* change.

If I were going the wrong way in the middle of a marathon, and I realized my mistake, would I keep going? No! I would immediately turn around! Why? Because I would have lost valuable time and precious energy and strength, and it would be much harder for me to finish the marathon because of this extra distance and added time. I wouldn't stay on the wrong course because no matter how long I ran there, I would never reach the finish line. And yet, for many who have made a moral mistake, a little voice keeps saying: "You blew it. You can't change. No one will ever know anyway." To you I would say, Don't believe it. As it says in *For the Strength of Youth,* "Satan wants you to think that you cannot repent, but that is absolutely not true" (30). A return is always possible because of the Savior's Atonement.

President Monson has said to each of us who have made mistakes: "If any of you has slipped along the way, there are those who will help you to once again become clean and worthy. Your bishop or branch president is anxious and willing to help and will, with understanding and compassion, do all within his power to assist you in the repentance process, that you may once again stand in righteousness before the Lord" ("Examples of Righteousness," 65–66).

Some of you have been abused and are victims of the sinful acts of others. As Mormon said, you have been deprived "of that which [is] most dear and precious above all things, . . . chastity and virtue" (Moroni 9:9). Please know that you are not to blame, for you have not sinned and repentance is not required. Because of the Savior's Atonement, healing is possible. The Savior suffered not only for our sins and imperfections, but He also took upon Himself our sorrows (see Alma 7:11). Through His infinite Atonement He will heal you and give you peace. Run to Him. Because of our Savior's Atonement, God the Father will hear your prayers. He will answer through the Holy Ghost and others who will be placed in your path.

I am so grateful for this doctrine and for the principle of repentance. Without it, none of us could ever return to our heavenly home pure and worthy to dwell in the presence of God the Father and our Savior, Jesus Christ. I am grateful for the restoration of priesthood power on the earth in these latter days that enables us to receive the help we need to return to virtue. This power also enables us to remain "unspotted from the world" (Doctrine and Covenants 59:9) as we partake of the sacrament worthily. Each week as we renew our covenants, we promise to keep His commandments, to take His name upon us, and to always remember Him. And He, in turn, promises that we can always have His Spirit to be with us (see Doctrine and Covenants 20:77, 79).

In a world that is so enticing and so appealing, it is imperative for each of us to receive, recognize, and rely on the guidance of the Holy Ghost. This wondrous gift will show each of us "all things [that we] should do" (2 Nephi 32:5). That is an absolute promise because the Holy Ghost is a member of the Godhead. Some of His roles are to teach, testify, comfort, and warn. This precious gift also purifies and sanctifies. Thus the Holy Ghost and virtue are inextricably connected. We can be purified "by fire and by the Holy Ghost" (2 Nephi 31:17), which will bring us closer to the point where "we have no more disposition to do evil, but to do good continually" (Mosiah 5:2).

Second, be careful about your choice of friends. In today's technological society, we may spend more time with nonhuman companions than we do with our peers. Although we may be very careful about our *human* companions, sometimes we give little thought to the other companions that we allow to influence us. Media of any kind can be a very powerful social influencer. We have all been given three precious gifts for our mortal experience. These include our body, our agency, and our time. If Satan can entice us to use our time in unfocused or unproductive or—even worse—nonvirtuous pursuits and then deceive us into believing that if we do this in private our actions don't affect anyone, he is victorious. "If there is anything virtuous, lovely, or of good report or praiseworthy, we [must] seek after these things" (Articles of Faith 1:13).

Seek the companionship of *virtuous* friends, not *virtual* friends. Remember, "virtue loveth virtue [and] light cleaveth unto light" (Doctrine and Covenants 88:40).

Third, enter a program of strict training. When training for a marathon, one has to have a strict training plan in order to be prepared to go the distance. This same concept applies to life. We are in the run of our life, and there must be a strict training plan. The components of success in this plan include things we will do *every single day,* without fail, in order to invite the Spirit's companionship into our life. They will be different for each of us but will always include daily prayer. Our Heavenly Father hears our prayers, and He will answer them. I testify that that is true. Our challenge is to be in a place where we can hear and recognize the answers.

Strict training should also include daily reading of the Book of Mormon. Joseph Smith said that "a man would get nearer to God by abiding by its precepts, than by any other book" (*History of the Church,* 4:461). This record is for us in this last dispensation. The Book of Mormon will increase our faith in Jesus Christ, and it is through our faith that we will be able to withstand temptation.

PRESS FORWARD—DON'T GET DISCOURAGED!

Let me add just one more suggestion to this list: "Press forward with . . . a perfect brightness of hope" (2 Nephi 31:20). Don't get discouraged! Our journey will be challenging at times.

As I have studied the scriptures, it has become increasingly clear to me that the Lord takes His chosen people out of their comfort zones again and again and tutors them on the things that really matter. For example, on the first leg of the Jaredites' journey, they landed on a beach, and they stayed there for four years. They were really in a comfort zone! In fact, they became so comfortable that they forgot to call upon the Lord. But the Lord had a different experience in mind for them. He chastened the brother of Jared for three hours. He told him in advance that the next leg of the journey would be difficult—that he would be submerged in the depths of the sea and driven by the winds. But He also reassured him with six beautiful words: "I prepare you against these things" (Ether 2:25). The Lord will prepare you, and He will prepare a way for you!

Sometimes I think we totally underestimate the great blessings we might have and the knowledge we might gain if we were willing to move out of our comfort zones. Perhaps that is why Nephi observed:

"Wo be unto him that is at ease in Zion!

"Wo be unto him that crieth: All is well!

"Yea, wo be unto him that hearkeneth unto the precepts of men, and denieth the power of God, and the gift of the Holy Ghost!" (2 Nephi 28:24–26).

It has been said that we are becoming a generation of spectators and critics. One of my favorite quotations, from President Theodore Roosevelt, says: "It is not the critic who counts; not the man who points out how the strong man stumbles, or where the doer of deeds could have done them better. The credit belongs to the man who is actually in the arena, whose face is marred by dust and sweat and blood; who strives valiantly; who errs, and comes short again and again, because there is no effort without error and shortcoming; but who does actually strive to do the deeds; who

knows the great enthusiasms, the great devotions; who spends himself in a worthy cause; who at the best knows in the end the triumph of high achievement, and who at the worst, if he fails, at least fails while daring greatly, so that his place shall never be with those cold and timid souls who knew neither victory nor defeat" (in Edmunds, *Colonel Roosevelt*, 47).

Do not be just a spectator or a critic. You didn't do that in the premortal realm. You weren't neutral then. You stood firm. Do not allow the very voices who cry for tolerance to not tolerate you or your view. This is the arena where all that you defended and chose *then* is taking place *now.* Do not get tired or distracted or disqualified! Be willing to step out of your comfort zone and "press forward with . . . a perfect brightness of hope" (2 Nephi 31:20).

VIRTUE BRINGS THE BLESSINGS OF ETERNITY

The words of Doctrine and Covenants section 121 are for those who are called and chosen and who endure valiantly. They are for each one of us in these trying days, just as they were for Joseph Smith and the Saints in those trying days of the early Church: "Let virtue garnish thy thoughts unceasingly; then shall thy confidence wax strong in the presence of God [and] the Holy Ghost shall be thy constant companion" (vv. 45–46).

When we are virtuous, we are promised that we shall confidently stand in His presence—holy and like Him. We are promised priesthood power, the very power of godliness, because we are virtuous. We are promised the constant companionship of the

Holy Ghost, who testifies, directs, warns, comforts, and sanctifies. And finally, we are promised that we shall have eternal life, the greatest of all God's gifts. We will be like Him—pure even as He is pure.

The journey to Zion—the pure in heart—will take everything you and I have. I pray that each one of us will have the desire and strength to move out of our comfort zones as we prepare for the run of our lives and, like Agnes Caldwell, reach up and take the Master's hand. His promise is for each of us: "I will go before your face. I will be on your right hand and on your left, and my Spirit shall be in your hearts, and mine angels round about you, to bear you up" (Doctrine and Covenants 84:88). There may be some steep hills ahead, but our Lord and Savior, Jesus Christ, has promised to climb with us every step of the way.

Chapter 2

STRICT TRAINING

A Foundation for Virtue

When you are preparing to run a race, particularly a marathon, one of the first things to do is to work out a plan for training. You don't just decide one day that you'll go out and run twenty-six miles. You need a foundation of many smaller workouts, strength training, aerobic exercise, and practice runs.

When I think of foundations, I think of a photograph I once saw of three sheds, two of which were leaning on the third and smallest shed. The accompanying caption read: "You need to be strong when you are the last one to take a stand." We too need to be strong. As we are faithful and righteous, others will look to us for support and strength.

Helaman describes how this is

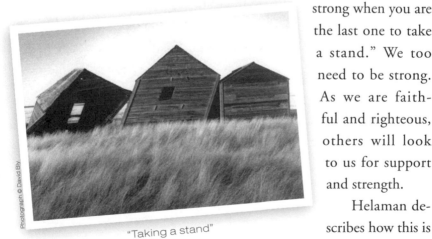

"Taking a stand"

possible: "And now, . . . remember, remember that it is upon the rock of our Redeemer, who is Christ, the Son of God, that ye must build your foundation; . . . which is a sure foundation, a foundation whereon if men build they cannot fall" (Helaman 5:12).

In our quest for virtue, we are building each day on the foundation of Christ as well as on the foundation of strength and testimony laid by those who went before us. I gained a new appreciation for that foundation some years ago when my husband and I visited Nauvoo. As we walked through the old pioneer cemetery searching for the grave of an ancestor, Zina Baker Huntington, I was touched by the peaceful solitude and spirit I felt. I walked through the trees and read the names on the gravestones, many of them children and families. I wept as my heart was turned to our forefathers, many of whom had joined the Church and come to Nauvoo. In my mind I asked many questions: Why did they leave their comfortable homes and families? Why did they suffer persecution, sickness, even death? Why did they sacrifice all that they had to come to this place and build a temple? They hardly had shelter, and yet they were building a temple! Why did they do it? And when the temple was nearly completed, how could they leave it behind? As I sat silently contemplating this scene, the answer came forcefully yet softly to my mind and heart: "We did this for you."

Those words, "We did this for you," reminded me that our ancestors, along with many other faithful Saints, sacrificed everything because of their testimonies and faith in Jesus Christ. They knew that the gospel had been restored to the earth once more and that they were led by a prophet of God. They knew that the Book of Mormon was true and understood its message and witness. They knew that through the restoration of priesthood keys, families could be sealed together for eternity through holy priesthood ordinances. They sacrificed everything to build the foundation for past and future generations to have access to the eternal blessings of the gospel.

On a pier in Copenhagen, Denmark, is a bronze statue of a young woman named Kristina. Kristina stands looking out to sea toward her goal to join the Saints in Zion. The wind is blowing against her fiercely, but she does not look back. She is steadfast as she presses forward doing a very hard thing, but one she knows to be right (see Stevenson, "Church marks 150 years in Scandinavia"). I love that statue, for to me Kristina represents my own Scandinavian great-great-grandmother who chose to join the Church amid great resistance. I am grateful for her courage and testimony. On her choice that day rested not only my eternal destiny but also the destiny of generations.

Fast-forward through those generations, and view with me my father as a young boy helping my grandfather on the farm. When he was about twelve, he suffered a serious accident while working on the farm. He and his younger brother, Ivan, were preparing a field with a team of horses and a harrow. My father was somehow pulled from the seat and fell to the ground, and one of the spikes or tines on the harrow penetrated his hip. He was dragged a long distance by the team of horses. When the horses stopped, my father lay still with multiple cuts, serious damage to his leg, and a broken hip. He lay motionless and in pain for weeks

My father,
Melvin Schwartz

in bed in the care of his mother, as she did the best she could to care for her son. The entire family united in fasting and prayer. And his father, William, exercised his priesthood power to bless his son with recovery. That was all they had—the power of prayer, the power of the priesthood, and the power of faith. After many weeks and many prayers, my father's wounds and hip healed and his life was spared. His recovery was miraculous. Through it all he did not get an infection, which could have taken his life, and his hip finally healed enough that he began to walk with the aid of little homemade crutches. He was so eager not to miss school that he rode sidesaddle to the little one-room schoolhouse for five or so miles each day. His brother, Ivan, led the horse and walked on foot beside my father.

As I have visited that dry farm in Daniels, Idaho, and stood on that road, I have wondered at the faith of my father's family, who relied on the power of prayer and priesthood. I have also marveled at the nurturing care of a loving mother, the righteousness of a father, and the love and dedication of a younger brother. I believe that at the young age of twelve, my father came to know God. This difficult experience refined and defined my father, and he dedicated his life to the Lord. I grew up knowing that my father loved the Lord, and so I did too. I knew that prayers were answered by a loving Heavenly Father because my father knew it. I knew that miracles were possible as we have faith and live worthy to receive promised blessings because of my father's miraculous recovery. Today, because my father taught me these things, his righteous influence lives on in my children and my grandchildren. It has provided for us a strong foundation of faith.

Other stories of miracles, large and small, experienced by our family have added to that foundation. One such event occurred in the life of my Grandfather Martin in the days of the Great Depression. Jobs and money were scarce. My grandfather had a family of four—three boys and one girl, my mother. It was nearing Thanksgiving, and the family had no money for a turkey for the Thanksgiving meal. My grandfather was called in for a day of work at Perry Monument. He was a stonemason by trade and created beautiful grave markers.

But he also received a call from the bishop, with whom he served as a counselor, to go to the ward house to do some work critical to the progress of the building's construction. My grandfather told the bishop he had to work, as there was no money for a turkey for the Thanksgiving meal. But upon reflection, he decided instead to do as he had been asked by the Lord's servant. And so he went to the ward to work for the day. My grandmother was not very happy about this decision. It meant no Thanksgiving turkey.

All day my grandfather did the necessary work, along with several others. At the close of the day, as he was gathering his tools, he heard a noise in the organ loft. He went to inspect, and there on the rafters of the organ loft was perched a large wild turkey. Needless to say, that turkey couldn't escape my grandfather, and my family enjoyed a sumptuous meal on Thanksgiving Day, returning thanks to the Lord who provided that miraculous blessing. My grandfather's story has become a part of a foundation of faith that has been passed from generation to generation. I am so grateful for his dedication to the Lord and for his faith. Because of him, I know, as did Nephi, that the Lord provides the way for us to accomplish the thing He commands us (see 1 Nephi 3:7). And in the process, He blesses us abundantly.

I remember other miracles. When I was young, one morning the phone at our house rang and someone said, "Bishop, come quick! The building is on fire."

My father ran from the house, dressing on the way up to the corner. Until that day, I had never seen my father cry. He burst through the firemen and ran up the stairs, only to see his office filled with flames. His first thought was for the records, and so he ran inside and got what he could and threw them out the window. Then he ran to the chapel and threw open each of the beautiful stained-glass windows so the pressure and intense heat would not make them burst. Then he was forced by smoke and heat to come outside and watch—and cry.

After the fire was extinguished, we helped to salvage what was left. I remember mourning over the blackened walls and ceiling in the chapel, but rejoicing that the windows were saved. Mostly I remember the miracle—the records that were in the bishop's office were burned around the edges, but the vital information was still intact and could be read. This was a true miracle, and I knew it. Again, I felt Heavenly Father very near.

When we are in training for our own race, it is helpful to *remember.* Remember the miracles we have witnessed. Remember those who have gone before us. Remember their faith, their testimonies, and their willingness to sacrifice to build the kingdom here on the earth. And remember that the Lord's tender mercies are upon all who love Him and seek to do His will. "The tender mercies of the Lord are over all those whom he hath chosen, because of their faith" (1 Nephi 1:20).

As we learn more about the faith of those who have gone before us, we can better understand those with whom we have joined hands in bearing witness of the Savior and helping to establish His kingdom. We can determine to live more righteously as faithful disciples of the Lord Jesus Christ.

As we read the Book of Mormon, we get a picture of the firm foundation that was laid by the fathers for the succeeding generations. Nephi built on Lehi's faith. The sons of Mosiah built on the faith of their father. Their success was a result of following the pattern set by their forefathers. In fact, Mosiah's son Ammon was literally sustained by the faith of his father, who was told by the Lord in answer to his prayers for his son: "It shall be unto him according to *thy* faith" (Alma 19:23; emphasis added). The accomplishments of the sons of Mosiah were partly because of their father.

As Isaac Newton humbly remarked about his own unprecedented accomplishments, the ability to see further often comes from "standing on the shoulders of Giants" (in Westfall, *Never at Rest: A Biography of Isaac Newton,* 274). Many times in the Book of Mormon, the sons reached new heights by building on the firm foundation their fathers had laid. To stand on the shoulders of one's parents is something for which children today should strive. President Brigham Young counseled the Saints:

"You may say to yourselves, 'If I can do as well as my parents, I think I shall do well, and be as good as I want to be; and I should not strive to excel them.' But if you do your duty you will far excel them in everything that is good . . . for this is your privilege, and it becomes your duty" (*Journal of Discourses,* 2:18).

In a broadcast for "Music and the Spoken Word," Lloyd D. Newell said: "When all is well and life is good, we tend to forget those who have made our present comforts possible: the teachers, parents, ancestors, and others who've sacrificed in our behalf. We drive on roads we didn't build, or we eat food we didn't grow—we all enjoy benefits and blessing that have come from the work of others. How often do we pause to acknowledge this?" ("Lest We Forget," April 2, 2006).

When we choose to remember those who have made our blessings possible, we appreciate those blessings much more.

Some years ago, I was invited to speak at the sesquicentennial celebration of the Ogden Fourth Ward building. It was a time for remembering some of the foundations of my own faith. My Grandfather Martin, who was a counselor in the bishopric when the building was being constructed, reflected: "It seems almost paradoxical that a community in which there were no wealthy men, and few that could be considered even well-to-do, should have undertaken in the befogged [Depression days] of August 1929 the erection of a ward chapel that was to cost over a hundred thousand dollars. But every member of the ward unselfishly rallied to the cause, the men and boys doing the manual labor and the women of the Relief Society furnishing the meals and refreshments."

Grandfather Martin

My mother recalls taking a dime with her to Primary each week to buy a brick for the building. I wonder how many bricks were purchased with children's contributions. To complete the building, it required seven hundred and fifty thousand bricks, fourteen carloads of cement, many hundred yards of gravel, thousands of feet of lumber, and eight years. It required vision, patience, strength, calluses—but mostly it required faith.

As I studied the records left by my father and grandfather, memories flooded into my consciousness that were long since forgotten. My growing up in the Ogden Fourth Ward became vivid. This was the place where my testimony was formed and strengthened. I remember:

- Dances in the cultural hall and dancing with my bishop father at the daddy-daughter dates, feeling that he was the cutest and best father there.

- The crimson carpet and the red and black velvet choir seats.

- Road shows, and just waiting for my turn on the stage.

- The Scout room, which always seemed like forbidden territory.

- The cloak room, filled with beautiful coats and boots and the clanging of hangers after and before meetings.

- The safe, where precious things like records and sacrament trays were stored.

- The gym doors that I hid behind when someone in my Primary class told me who Santa really was.

- Learning to crochet and to knit and to embroider—and writing the words on linen: "I will greet the day with a song."

- Counting the grapes on the ceiling during long meetings as a way to stay occupied and sit still.

- Relief Society bazaars on the lawn and Primary carnivals and parades.

- The baptismal font and the mural of John the Baptist baptizing Jesus, and the overwhelming feeling that I was about to have that same privilege.

- Hands on my head to confirm me a member of the Church and to bestow on me the very precious gift of the companionship of the Holy Ghost—which gift I cherish.

- Interviews with the bishop—my father.

- The sacrament—and the ceramic plaque above the sacrament table reminding me of the Last Supper and of Jesus and His disciples.

- The tower room where I always went to pray—the feeling I always received that Heavenly Father was very near and loved me.

So many vivid memories. So precious now. So important in the development of my testimony. More than what I was taught, what I remember was a feeling, a knowledge that everyone knew me and expected great things. I wasn't the only one who felt this way. We were like one big, happy family, and isn't that what it's all about, really—to love and lift and care for one another?

"Every human action gains in honour, in grace, in all true magnificence," said nineteenth-century poet and art critic John Ruskin, "by its regard to things that are to come. . . . Therefore, when we build, let us think that we build forever. Let it not be for present delight, nor for present use alone; let it be such work as our descendants will thank us for, and let us think, as we lay stone on stone, that a time is to come when those stones will be held sacred because our hands have touched them, and that men will say as they look upon the labour and wrought substance of them, 'See! this our fathers did for us'" (*The Seven Lamps of Architecture,* 171–72).

We honor the past and we look to the future. We acknowledge sacrifice and hard work and dedication to the purposes of the Lord. We acknowledge each small part that has made up the whole of our faith. Well might we ask ourselves: "What can I do today to build on the legacy of faith and sacrifice that went before me? What must I do?" Perhaps this very day will be a day of re-dedication for us personally for the cause in which we so valiantly fought in the premortal realms. For it was there that the firm foundation was laid—"a foundation whereon if men build they cannot fall" (Helaman 5:12).

I thank those who went before us and laid this firm foundation. I thank them for their sacrifice, for their willingness to put first things first. I thank them for the depth of their testimony. I thank them for the lessons, for their example, and mostly for their faith.

Today, as then, He is near. He is mindful of us. Today, as then, He hears and answers our prayers. Today, as then, He works through us to touch and teach and bless. Today, as then, there are those among us who are willing to give all they possess for the furtherance of His work on the earth. Today, as then, to those who sacrifice and give their all comes the joy that is spoken of in the scriptures, a joy that passes all understanding. As we gain strength from our foundational training, centered on the Lord Jesus Christ, we will be truly prepared to run a good race.

Chapter 3

Starting Out

Modesty, the Essential Root of Virtue

We have spoken of the foundation of training that must precede any race. Now, as we stand at the starting line, there is another key principle that must be firmly stored in our minds and hearts if we are to be successful in our quest for virtue. That principle is modesty.

When we speak of modesty, I am reminded of what Tevye, a character in the musical *Fiddler on the Roof,* said when he spoke of his beloved city of Anatevka: "In Anatevka, everyone knows who he is and what God expects him to do." For me, that is the bottom line of any discussion on modesty.

Modesty is often talked of in terms of dress and appearance, but modesty encompasses much more than the outward appearance. It is a condition of the heart. It is an outward manifestation of an inner knowledge and commitment. It is an expression that we understand our identity as children of God. It is an expression that we know what He expects us to do. It is a declaration of our covenant keeping. A question in the *For the Strength of Youth* booklet really is the question each of us must consider: "Am I living the way the Lord wants me to live?" (40).

Speaking to members of the ancient Church, the Apostle Peter said: "But ye are a chosen generation, a royal priesthood, an holy nation, a peculiar people; that ye should shew forth the praises of him who hath called you out of darkness into his marvellous light" (1 Peter 2:9).

He clearly defined our identity. And his use of the word *peculiar* did not mean "odd." It meant "special."

In the Book of Mormon the Lord's people are described in this way: "Ye are the children of the prophets; and ye are of the house of Israel; and ye are of the covenant which the Father made with your fathers" (3 Nephi 20:25). Elder Russell M. Nelson of the Twelve said, "Once we know who we are and the royal lineage of which we are a part, our actions and our direction in life will be more appropriate to our inheritance" (*Perfection Pending,* 208). Even the Young Women Theme reminds us that we are "daughters of our Heavenly Father who loves us."

When we truly know that we are children of God, when we have an understanding of our divine nature, it will be reflected in our countenance, our appearance, and our actions.

Several years ago, a dear friend of mine married in the Salt Lake Temple. She was a convert to the Church from India and her entire family came for her wedding. They were not members of the Church, but waited patiently outside for the wedding to end and the bride to exit the temple. They were dressed in native Indian attire and looked beautiful. When they walked onto the temple grounds, all eyes were upon them. The thing I noticed most was how elegantly they moved and carried themselves and how modest each was. They were not apologetic for their appearance even though it made them stand out in the crowd. They simply knew who they were and were not ashamed. I observed how beautiful they were. The women seemed almost queenly in their attitude and demeanor. In their actions, movements, and conversation they were dignified and lovely. I thought how wonderful it would be if every young woman and woman in the Church had that same attitude: an attitude of understanding something deeper on the inside that was reflected on the outside.

President Gordon B. Hinckley said, "Of all the creations of the Almighty, there is none more beautiful, none more inspiring than a lovely daughter of God who walks in virtue with an understanding of why she should do so, who honors and respects her body as a thing sacred and divine, who cultivates her mind and constantly enlarges the horizon of her understanding, who nurtures her spirit with everlasting truth" ("Our Responsibility to Our Young Women," 11). Women who know this know much more than how to dress. They know how to live, and they have the courage they need to avoid the moral decline of the world.

Clear back in the early days of the Church, President Brigham Young desired that the women of the Church reflect their true identity. Visualize this setting with me for a moment. It was 1869, and the prophet, Brigham Young, had become concerned. He was concerned about his daughters and their somewhat worldly interests and actions. He was worried about a general trend toward materialism, commercialism, and sophistication among the Church members; indeed, it seemed to him that his daughters reflected that trend. So he assembled his family in the Lion House parlor for a meeting. He looked into the faces of his lovely daughters and said, "All Israel are looking to my family and watching the example set by my . . . children. For this reason I desire to organize my own family first into a society for the promotion of habits of order, thrift, industry, and charity; and, above all things, I desire them to retrench from their extravagance in dress, . . . in your speech, wherein you have been guilty of silly . . . speeches and light-mindedness of thought. Retrench in everything that is bad and worthless, and improve in everything that is good and beautiful" (in Gates, *History of the Young Ladies' Mutual Improvement Association,* 8, 9–10).

We don't often hear the word *retrench* in our day. The dictionary defines *retrench* to mean: "to cut down or reduce . . . curtail, . . . to cut off or out" (*Webster's New World College Dictionary,* s.v. "retrench"). This definition helps us to understand the last sentence of Brigham Young's declaration. He desired his daughters to curtail and diminish in everything that was bad and worthless and to improve in that which was good and beautiful.

In the Doctrine and Covenants we are admonished, "Arise and shine forth, that thy light may be a standard for the nations" (115:5). Perhaps it is again time to "retrench."

In recent times, President Gordon B. Hinckley issued a similar call to the women of the Church. He said: "It is so tremendously important that the women of the Church stand strong and immovable for that which is correct and proper under the plan of the Lord. . . . If they will be united and speak with one voice, their strength will be incalculable. We call upon the women of the Church to stand together for righteousness. They must begin in their own homes. They can teach it in their classes. They can voice it in their communities. They must be the teachers and the guardians of their daughters." He continued: "I see this as the one bright shining hope in a world that is marching toward self-destruction" ("Standing Strong and Immovable," 20).

President Hinckley asked of both youth and adults: "If we are to hold up this Church as an ensign to the nations and a light to the world, we must take on more of the luster of the life of Christ individually and in our own personal circumstances. In standing for the right, we must not be fearful of the consequences. We must never be afraid. Said Paul to Timothy:

"'For God hath not given us the spirit of fear; but of power, and of love, and of a sound mind.

"'Be not thou therefore ashamed of the testimony of our Lord' (2 Timothy 1:7–8)" ("An Ensign to the Nations," 84).

Modesty, therefore, is more than the way we dress. It truly reflects our testimony and the condition of our hearts. It is an outward manifestation of an inward knowledge and commitment. It begins with the little things. It begins with knowing who we are and what God expects us to do.

Are we willing to do what is expected of us? To begin with, are we willing to do what it takes to dress modestly?

Dressing modestly can be a challenge. As President Hinckley taught: "We cannot accept that which has become common in the world. Yours, as members of this Church, is a higher standard and more demanding. . . .

"Modesty in dress and manner will assist in protecting against temptation. It may be difficult to find modest clothing, but it can be found with enough effort. I sometimes wish every girl had access to a sewing machine and training in how to use it. She could then make her own attractive clothing. I suppose this is an unrealistic wish. But I do not hesitate to say that you can be attractive without being immodest. You can be refreshing and buoyant and beautiful in your dress and in your behavior. Your appeal to others will come of your personality, which is the sum of your individual characteristics. Be happy. Wear a smile. Have fun. But draw some rigid parameters, a line in the sand, as it were, beyond which you will not go" ("Stay on the High Road," 114).

President Spencer W. Kimball suggested we establish a "style of our own" ("On My Honor," 3). And as wickedness progresses in the world, we may have to do just that. We cannot lead if we are like the world. Instead of spending our energy and our money to look like the world, perhaps we should set a pattern that they may choose to follow. We must have the courage and the gospel understanding to be modest. Modesty will not only set us apart from the world, but it will also protect us.

For the Strength of Youth admonishes us, "Never lower your dress standards for any occasion. Doing so sends the message that you are using your body to get attention and approval and that modesty is important only when it is convenient" (15). Are we willing to obey the standard of modesty, "at all times and in all things, and in all places" (Mosiah 18:9)?

Modesty is more than hemlines, necklines, and revealing clothing. It is the appropriate dress for the appropriate setting. It is caring to dress appropriately to show respect for people, places, and settings. We hear more and more concern from our Brethren about excessive casualness in our dress. "In your attempt to follow the styles and be casual, do not offend good taste. When we go to worship the Lord, we ought to be dressed in our finest, cleanest, and best" (Tuttle, "Your Mission Preparation," 71).

When we understand modesty, we know how to be appropriate in any given situation. We know how to dress to run a marathon as well as how to dress to attend a priesthood ordinance. We understand that wearing a white shirt and tie to pass the sacrament is more, much more, than a rule. We invite the companionship of the Spirit by the small things we do that demonstrate not only our attitude but also our understanding.

One year, the choir that had been invited to provide the music for the Young Women general meeting had a dress rehearsal in the Conference Center on a Saturday morning. Families were invited to attend. As I arrived, I noticed a family reverently waiting in the seats for the practice to begin. Each of the young boys had on a freshly ironed white shirt and tie, and the little girls wore their Sunday dresses. The mother and father were neatly dressed as well. As I shook the oldest boy's hand, I said, "I compliment you on the way you are dressed on this early Saturday morning. I can tell that you understand and have been taught some things that it takes a lot of people all their lives to realize." He flashed his mother a sheepish look, and she gave him that knowing look that said, "I told you so."

Mothers play a tremendous role in the modesty of their children. Mothers teach modesty in the home and model it through their example. Some say, "My daughter is a good girl. I don't want to make an issue of her tight clothing or skimpy T-shirts." They say, "I won't die on that hill." It is not about hills; it's about hearts. It is not about confrontation; it is about covenants. These are battles in which we should be engaged because modesty has moral implications. This is a different world from the one in which we grew up. By encouraging our daughters to be trendy, we may unknowingly be putting them at great risk. Are we more concerned about popularity than purity?

In 2004, I visited with Liriel Domiciano, a young woman from Brazil who has an extraordinary voice. Her talent has made her famous in Brazil. She insists on performing in modest attire. During an eight-month engagement on one Brazilian television program, Liriel wore her Young Womanhood Recognition medal-

Photograph by Deb Gehris. © by Intellectual Reserve, Inc.

Singer Liriel Domiciano

lion as a symbol of her values. When I asked her what kept her strong, she replied, "My mother is my protector." As mothers, we simply must be our daughters' protectors. We must start early. We must set the example as we dress to generously meet temple standards. We can teach these standards to our daughters and help them as they anticipate and prepare for their own temple attendance. We must never compromise those standards in order that our daughters might be popular or accepted by those with not only worldly standards but worldly intentions.

Here is a specific list of things we can do to protect our daughters and young women:

- Seek answers in the scriptures. The scriptures can help us find the answer to every question or problem.

- Know the doctrine and teach it. The doctrine is the WHY—the rules are the HOW. Our youth must understand both.

- Study the *For the Strength of Youth* pamphlet, which contains twenty-three ways to qualify for the companionship of the Holy Ghost. We simply must have this guidance in today's world.

- Teach them their eternal identity. My mother always called out when I left the house, "Remember who you are and what we stand for."

- Help them gain skills such as sewing, hemming, even sewing on a button. These build bonds between a mother and daughter.

- Seek experiences with the Spirit. In your home, pray, read scriptures, and listen to sacred music.

- Serve others. Don't let them base their identity on designer labels. "Pretty is as pretty does."

- Teach covenant-keeping and obedience above worldly acceptance.

- Live what you know—be an example.

- Live the standards generously, not teetering on the edge of the line.

Modesty is a daily standard that, if lived, has eternal promise. Modesty extends to our actions, our speech, our attitudes, thoughts, even our desires. Our modesty is a reflection of our desire to follow a prophet of God. I repeat: *being modest is more than how we dress.* Modesty is an outward manifestation of our inward commitment and understanding.

We have a dear friend who worked as a gardener at the Oakland Temple. He shared with us the following insight, which he also related in the *Ensign* several years ago: "Our temples are kept beautiful on the outside. I spent many, many hours grooming the temple grounds—weeding, watering, planting flowers, doing all I could to make the exterior reflect the sacred spirit inside the Lord's holy house. Surely the Lord expects us to groom and care for our physical tabernacles also—not as the world does, but in order that the Spirit of the Lord may find a fit sanctuary to dwell with our own spirits" (Tanner, "To Clothe a Temple," 47). The outward appearance of the temple and the grounds reflect the inner spirit and beauty of the temple. So it is with us.

Paul said, "Know ye not that your body is the temple of the Holy Ghost which is in you, which ye have of God, and ye are not your own? For ye are bought with a price: therefore glorify God in your body, and in your spirit, which are God's" (1 Corinthians 6:19–20).

Our purpose in coming to earth was to gain a body with which to have experience and joy, and to exercise our agency. Our bodies are a precious gift from a loving Heavenly Father. We are made in His image. Our bodies are the instruments of our agency and the receptacles of our spirits. There is only one to a customer. It is precious. When Adam and Eve had partaken of the fruit in the Garden of Eden and become mortal and subject to temptation, they covered themselves with fig leaves. Later, a loving Heavenly Father, in an act of total mercy, placed a covering over their bodies in the form of coats of skins (see Genesis 3:21). He did this not only to protect them from the elements but also to protect them from man's fallen nature (see Tanner, "To Clothe a Temple," 44). Consequently, personal modesty is evidence that we understand that our bodies are sacred.

Our modesty—in fact, all of our standards and our willingness to live them—are a reflection of our covenants as members of the Church. When I was a new Young Women general board member, Elder Robert D. Hales helped me to really understand what my baptismal covenant meant. He said, "When you were baptized, you stepped out of the world and into the kingdom." He said that when we truly understand this, it changes everything. It did for me. Elder Hales's teaching awakened in me a desire to reflect in every way that I am a woman of covenant. Each time I partake of the sacrament, I remember that I promised to always remember Him. I see myself literally stepping across a line out of an ever-darkening world and into the brightness of the kingdom. Again and again I ask myself, "Am I living the way the Lord wants me to live?"

Our covenants provide protection, direction, and focus. They enable us to navigate a very turbulent world guided by His Spirit. When we are keeping our covenants, it is extremely difficult to keep one foot in the world and the other in the kingdom.

Some young women in Kansas received a lesson on modesty and its relationship to covenants and keeping them. They thought about what they could do. They remembered that the converts of Ammon, former Lamanites, had repented of their warlike ways and covenanted with the Lord. They had buried their swords and weapons of war in connection with their covenant. These young women decided that they would go to their closets and take out any immodest clothing. But they didn't want to be the cause of anyone else being immodest by giving those items away, so they took their clothes out to the yard and buried them! Their outward actions reflected their inward desires. They desired to be covenant keepers.

When we are modest, we reflect in our outward actions and appearance that we understand what God expects us to do. We reflect that we are women of covenant. Our actions and appearance invite the companionship of the Holy Ghost, which, we are told, will "show unto you all things what ye should do" (2 Nephi 32:5). In the world in which we live, can we risk being without this sure compass and companion? The pressures of the world must not push us into places where the Spirit cannot dwell.

In our day prophets have again issued the call to young women and women to retrench, to arise, to be worthy of imitation. Our standards are clearly outlined for us and they carry with them infinitely great rewards. We are promised by prophets of God that if we live the standards, we "will be able to do [our] life's work with greater wisdom and skill and bear trials with greater courage. [We] will have the help of the Holy Ghost. [We] will feel good about [ourselves] and will be a positive influence in the lives of others. And [we] will be worthy to go to the temple to receive holy ordinances" (*For the Strength of Youth,* 2–3). What more could a woman want for her family or for herself?

The Book of Mormon people who assembled at the Waters

of Mormon were converted to the gospel. They were about to be baptized and enter into a covenant which included "stand[ing] as witnesses of God at all times and in all things, and in all places." When Alma asked them if they were willing to do this, "they clapped their hands for joy, and exclaimed: This is the desire of our hearts" (Mosiah 18:9, 11). Why was it their hearts' desire? Because, just as those people of Anatevka, they had been taught and understood who they really were and what God expected them to do. They wanted to change. They understood and wanted the promises. And they were willing to do whatever it took to have the blessing of the companionship of the Holy Ghost.

As daughters of God and women of covenant, we have stepped out of the world and into the kingdom. Now is the time to "Arise and shine forth, that [our] light may be a standard for the nations" (Doctrine and Covenants 115:5). May we hold that standard high as we embark on our eternal race.

Chapter 4

RUNNING THE LONG MILES

Living a Virtuous Life

I know a lot of people who say they cannot envision running a marathon because that kind of exercise is tedious to them. It is true that when you are in the middle of all those long miles, it sometimes seems as if the road will stretch on forever.

Life has moments like that as well. Sometimes the challenge to stick with it in trying to live virtuously seems unrewarding, unfulfilling, unremarkable. May I suggest that some of the most remarkable things that can happen to us actually happen when we are in the course of doing our very ordinary duties?

There are many ordinary days and events in the scriptures that led to extraordinary miracles. I think about an ordinary lad, perhaps sent out by his mother with five loaves and two fishes to sell. Or perhaps he was on his way home with those things, having been sent to purchase the family's daily groceries. Or perhaps it was the lunch his mother had sent with him for the day. At any rate, he was willing to give all that he had to the disciples of Christ—and an ordinary day became miraculous. An ordinary lad was part of an extraordinary miracle! Not only was *he* fed, but five thousand others and their spirits were fed the bread of life.

President James E. Faust explained: "It has been said that this church does not necessarily attract great people but more often makes ordinary people great. Many nameless people with gifts equal only to five loaves and two small fishes magnify their callings and serve without attention or recognition, feeding literally thousands" ("Five Loaves and Two Fishes," 5).

I think also of Naaman, the captain of the Syrian hosts, who was a leper. A little Israelite servant told Naaman's wife that there was a prophet in Israel who could heal him. Naaman came with his chariot and horses to the house of Elisha, who sent a messenger to instruct Naaman, an ordinary servant, carrying the words of the prophet: "Go and wash in Jordan seven times, and thy flesh shall come again to thee, and thou shalt be clean" (2 Kings 5:10). Here we have the captain of the Syrian hosts, being told to wash himself in a dirty, polluted river. He was offended by Elisha's instruction to wash in the Jordan. So he "went away in a rage" (2 Kings 5:12).

One of Naaman's servants with a wise head spoke with him and said: "If the prophet had bid thee do some great thing, wouldest thou not have done it? how much rather then, when he saith to thee, Wash, and be clean?" Naaman then repented and followed the counsel of the prophet. The leprosy disappeared, and "his flesh came again like unto the flesh of a little child, and he was clean" (2 Kings 5:13–14). "Some great thing" in this instance was extraordinarily simple and easy to do.

I think of a fourteen-year-old young man with a question who knelt in a grove of trees to pray, a simple act that has changed countless lives and blessed the whole earth. "From thence shall the gospel roll forth unto the ends of the earth, as the stone cut out of a mountain without hands shall roll forth, until it has filled the whole earth" (Doctrine and Covenants 65:2).

There are ordinary things we do every time we meet as Saints that turn out to make all the difference. At just about any given church meeting, we will:

- Sing together
- Pray together
- Gather together
- Laugh
- Make eye contact
- Smile
- Greet warmly
- Listen
- Answer questions
- Touch
- Suggest
- Testify

These are all ordinary things that create extraordinary results. They are the fruits of the Spirit! And we are told in the scriptures that "a little leaven leaveneth the whole lump" (Galatians 5:9).

The Lord asks us to reach out with kindness to others—in ordinary ways. President Henry B. Eyring says it this way: "He will, through you, touch the hearts of others. . . . And they will then, in turn, be touched and reach out to others, multiplying the effects of your investment of time and effort and faith" (*Because He First Loved Us*, 36).

The influence we can have on others who are running this race with us can be great, particularly in the long stretch of miles ahead of us. However, even when we have started the race with the greatest of intentions, it is possible for us to get discouraged, distracted, delayed, or disqualified, and so to fall away as the race progresses.

The parable of the ten virgins is one I have thought about deeply over the past few years. There is a painting of these ten virgins in the Conference Center in Salt Lake City, Utah. As I stand before it, I find the artist Walter Rane's depictions of the virgins in various states of preparedness simply stunning. Carved into the frame surrounding this painting are the words from the scripture in Matthew, "Five of them were wise." These words concern me. I wonder, "What happened? All of these women were members of the Church with the everlasting gospel in their hearts and testimonies in their souls. All were invited to the wedding celebration and came with their lamps burning! All were aware of the Second Coming of our Lord and Savior Jesus Christ."

In Doctrine and Covenants section 45 the Lord elaborates further on this parable. He tells us: "And at that day, when I shall come in my glory, shall the parable be fulfilled which I spake concerning the ten virgins.

"For they that are wise and have received the truth, and have taken the Holy Spirit for their guide, and have not been deceived, . . . shall abide the day" (vv. 56–57).

Within this section the Lord answers some of my questions. He describes the situations to come prior to His return to the earth and He gives the formula for abiding the day. He tells us that nothing really matters unless we "avoid being deceived" and unless we *have* taken the Holy Spirit for our guide. But He also tells us one more wonderful thing. He says, "Wherefore I give unto you . . . that ye may be prepared for the things to come. For verily I say unto you, that great things await you" (vv. 61–62). I testify this is so. Great things await us if we will continue to move forward on our course.

We must never forget that we are women of covenant. We are not women of the world. When we were confirmed members of the Church we were given the most precious gift that anyone could bestow upon us: the gift of the Holy Ghost. Imagine—a member of the Godhead to be with us, to comfort us, to teach us, and to direct our every action! This gift comes to us through covenant. As we make covenants with the Lord, He keeps His promises with us. He has promised that as we keep His commandments, we can "*always* have his Spirit to be with us" (Doctrine and Covenants 20:77; emphasis added).

The winner of the New York Marathon some years back was interviewed about his strategy for success in the race. I found his response simple and yet very profound. Juma Ikangaa replied simply, "The will to win means nothing without the will to prepare." Preparation is one way we can avoid deception. And the Lord has not left us alone to figure things out. The scriptures abound with instructions for personal, temporal, and spiritual preparation. He has said: "Seek ye diligently and teach one another words of wisdom; yea, seek ye out of the best books words of wisdom, seek learning even by study and also by faith; organize yourselves; prepare every needful thing, and establish a house, even a house of prayer, a house of fasting, a house of faith, a house of learning, a house of glory, a house of order, a house of God" (Doctrine and Covenants 109:7–8).

These spiritual preparation checklists are everywhere in the scriptures. As I study the scriptures, I'm not finding any that say watch lots of TV, play tennis every day, or shop till you drop. The kind of preparation the Lord is teaching us is the kind that will accumulate in our vessels and will light the way now and when He comes again.

I would like to suggest four things that we can do to have the Holy Spirit for our guide so that we will not be deceived as we proceed on our way through the long miles of our race. These things will help us continue to strive for the great things that await us. Great things await those who (1) work hard and study things out, (2) are focused and not easily distracted, (3) are obedient and avoid procrastination, (4) and consistently do simple, doable things.

1. Great things await those who work hard and study things out.

Qualities of spirituality do not come without effort. The sons of Mosiah "had waxed strong in the knowledge of the truth; for . . . they had searched the scriptures diligently, that they might know the word of God. But this is not all; they had given themselves to much prayer, and fasting; therefore they had the spirit of prophecy, and the spirit of revelation" (Alma 17:2–3).

Like any other talent with which we are blessed, we must constantly practice the talent of spirituality.

Oliver Cowdery was taught this principle when the Lord gave

him the formula for revelation and personal spiritual guidance. The Lord told Oliver:

"Behold, you have not understood; you have supposed that I would give it unto you when you took no thought save it was to ask me. But, behold, I say unto you, that you must study it out in your mind; then you must ask me if it be right, and if it is right I will cause that your bosom shall burn within you; therefore, you shall feel that it is right. But if it be not right you shall have no such feelings, but you shall have a stupor of thought" (Doctrine and Covenants 9:7–9).

This formula for receiving personal revelation came as *revelation* to me when I was a student at Brigham Young University. I had met a young man I really liked and we had spoken of marriage. But I didn't know if he was the right person. I went to a devotional that day after I had prayed and asked how to know and what to do. In the devotional, Elder A. Theodore Tuttle referred to these verses from the Doctrine and Covenants as the way to make every decision in our lives correctly. I didn't know I had to work to know! I thought I could just ask! But carefully following this guidance enabled me to make a critical decision correctly, and I ended up saying yes to that young man. I know what it feels like to have this burning witness. When we walk by the Spirit, we need never make a mistake.

The Holy Ghost speaks to us in other ways. Sometimes it is through a still small voice. Enos said that "the voice of the Lord came into my mind" (Enos 1:10).

We have a friend who was attacked by a grizzly bear while running on the trails in Jackson, Wyoming. The voice of the

Spirit came into his mind as an impression: "Play dead." He heeded that voice and was saved from death.

In order to discern this guidance, we too must *heed*. We must be paying attention. Learning to recognize the voice of the Spirit takes practice. This voice speaks in ways that are different from the voice of the world. Studying the scriptures and pondering them will help us become familiar with and recognize the voice of the Spirit. Many times the answers to my prayers come as I am reading the scriptures. It is as if the voice of the Lord Himself is speaking directly to me.

A few days prior to my calling to the Young Women general presidency, I was reading the scriptures. A sweet spirit filled our home and I was alone and still. I shall never forget the tutoring I received that morning in preparation for this new calling. I specifically remember these words:

"I will impart unto you of my Spirit, which shall enlighten your mind, which shall fill your soul with joy; And then shall ye know, or by this shall you know, all things whatsoever you desire of me, which are pertaining unto things of righteousness, in faith believing in me that you shall receive" (Doctrine and Covenants 11:13–14).

This scripture has been oil in my lamp and a light to me.

2. Great things await those who are focused and not easily distracted.

In the world there is so much distraction. Satan wants it to be that way. He creates so much noise that it is hard to be still and listen to the whisperings of the Spirit. And yet we must always remember that the guidance of the Spirit is *so* close—it is within whispering distance! The Lord reminds us: "be still and know that I am God" (Doctrine and Covenants 101:16).

I love the attitude of Nehemiah in the Old Testament. Nehemiah faced much opposition and open persecution as he began to rebuild the walls of fortification around Jerusalem. His record says that things got so bad that everybody who worked on the wall had one of his hands wrought in the work and the other holding a weapon (see Nehemiah 4:17). They didn't even stop building to change their clothes! When Sanballat tried to distract Nehemiah from this work by proposing a meeting on the plains of Ono, Nehemiah sent a message to this leader: "I am doing a great work, so that I cannot come down; why should the work cease, whilst I leave it, and come down to you?" (Nehemiah 6:3). Nehemiah did not allow himself to become distracted, and neither should we.

We, as young women and wives and mothers and women of covenant, are doing a great work and we have yet a great work to do. It is vital for us to remember that we are living in the dispensation of the fullness of times. We need to have focus and set priorities. Jesus taught about priorities when He said, "Seek not the things of this world but seek ye first to build up the kingdom of God, and to establish his righteousness, and all these things shall be added unto you" (JST, Matthew 6:38).

3. Great things await those who are obedient and do not procrastinate.

Procrastination is the opposite of obedience. Amulek taught that "this life is the time for men to prepare to meet God." Then he pleaded, "I beseech of you that ye do not procrastinate the day of your repentance until the end; for after this day of life, which is given us to prepare for eternity, behold, if we do not improve our time while in this life, then cometh the night of darkness wherein there can be no labor performed" (Alma 34:32–33).

The scriptures tell us one of the ways the Savior learned obedience: "Though he were a Son, yet learned he obedience by the things which he suffered" (Hebrews 5:8). As you suffer in this life, your suffering can bless your life and tutor you in obedience. I think of the men who volunteered to participate in Zion's Camp. In this effort to redeem Zion, some two hundred men traveled more than a thousand miles in the most trying circumstances under the personal leadership of the Prophet Joseph Smith.

The march over a thousand miles was the source of much suffering, and in the end their purpose was not achieved. But I believe the Lord's purpose was fulfilled. Through that experience those men were *prepared* to lead the Church. They learned obedience. At a conference held in February of 1835, the Quorum of the Twelve Apostles and the Seventy were chosen from the ranks of those who had served in Zion's Camp. These valiant brethren led the Church for the next fifty years.

Obedience develops as our faith grows.

Nephi was perfectly obedient to the Lord because he knew the Lord and trusted Him. Nephi knew that the Lord would not command him to do something without providing a way. Even in the final sentence of his record he states simply and unequivocally, "I must obey" (2 Nephi 33:15).

4. Great things await those who consistently do the simple, doable things.

By the simple, doable things I mean practices such as prayer, fasting, scripture study, temple attendance, and following the counsel of our prophets. Doing these things consistently opens the door for the Spirit to be our constant companion. Each prayer, each scripture read, each temple session attended adds oil to our lamps. President Spencer Kimball said that the oil in our lamps is accumulated a drop at a time and that it is an individual pursuit: "Fasting, family prayer, . . . studying the scriptures—each act of dedication and obedience is a drop added to our store. Deeds of kindness, payment of offerings and tithes, chaste thoughts and actions, marriage in the covenant for eternity—these, too, contribute importantly to the oil with which we can at midnight refuel our exhausted lamps" (*Faith Precedes the Miracle,* 255).

Our son-in-law suffered a major stroke at age twenty-eight. He had just graduated from medical school, and the future looked bright. Then in an instant everything changed. He was completely paralyzed on his right side and unable to talk. My daughter came to me one quiet evening in the hospital and said, "Mom, you didn't prepare me for this. I thought that if I was good and righteous and did everything I was told to do, all would be all right in my life. You didn't prepare me for this."

What Emi didn't know was that she *was* prepared and that she was not alone. Her preparation had come a drop at a time over years of obedience, scripture study, and righteous living. She had the Holy Spirit for her guide. He upheld her. He inspired her when critical, life-and-death decisions needed to be made. He led her through a very difficult time. I see her now still being upheld and directed through this quietly incredible power. It inspires her mind, it helps her see an eternal perspective, it helps her focus on positive improvement and blessings. The Holy Ghost has comforted, led, and guided her husband through a difficult recovery as well. This companionship has strengthened him and given him optimism and courage and determination. And as a family, we have witnessed miracles. Our daughter and her husband will come through this trial because they have taken the Holy Spirit for their guide.

Perhaps we never feel like we are totally prepared for some of the events we experience in life, but if we cultivate the Holy Ghost as our constant companion, we will be led, guided, and comforted and will feel peace and direction—even at midnight.

As we strive to be worthy and pure, the Holy Ghost will guide and bless our lives. The Lord has said, "Sanctify yourselves that your minds become single to God" (Doctrine and Covenants 88:68).

As we accumulate oil for our lamps, we become vessels. Paul says, "If a man . . . purge himself [of unworthiness], he shall be a vessel unto honour, sanctified, and meet for the master's use, and prepared unto every good work" (2 Timothy 2:21). And the Lord Himself tells us: "For they will hear my voice, and shall see me, and shall not be asleep, and shall abide the day of my coming; for they shall be purified, even as I am pure" (Doctrine and Covenants 35:21).

Through daily doing the simple, doable things, we will become vessels pure and holy and filled with light. We will carry the oil with us that will burn brightly for all to see. What we have become will shine forth and be a light to others. In the words of President Henry B. Eyring: "Your worthiness and your desire will shine in your face and your eyes" ("A Child and a Disciple," 31).

The Lord tells us in the Doctrine and Covenants: "Be faithful, praying always, having your lamps trimmed and burning, and oil with you, that you may be ready at the coming of the Bridegroom" (33:17). Each morning when I awaken, the words on that frame in the Conference Center go through my mind: "Five of them were wise." And I ask myself, Will I be wise today? Will the young women in the world be wise? Will my children and grandchildren be wise? And then I pray for the guidance of the Holy Ghost to help me and to help us all recognize the power of ordinary things, to work hard, to be focused and obedient, and to consistently do the simple, doable things that will enable us to participate in the "great things that await us."

And I remember the Lord's promise to each of us: "I, the Lord . . . will be a light unto them forever, that hear my words" (2 Nephi 10:14). As we move forward faithfully through the long, dark miles, His light will ever attend us.

Chapter 5

HITTING THE WALL

When Adversity Strikes

There is a phenomenon that occurs in some, if not most, runners who participate in a marathon. It is called "hitting the wall." It is caused when runners use up all of their physical reserves, and their bodies have run out of the carbohydrates needed to sustain intense physical activities like long-distance running.

I have experienced this kind of fatigue myself: a sudden, overwhelming sense of "I can't do this" that feels, literally, like I have run into a wall and have to stop. For me, it usually occurs at the mile that marks three times my daily training average.

When you hit the wall, it is helpful to have someone encouraging you and helping you to mentally overcome this physical sensation. And you will probably cross the finish line on sheer mental willpower—which, interestingly enough, makes your finish just that much more thrilling and victorious.

Hitting the wall is real, and the concept applies not just to marathon running but to some of the situations we all experience in life. Sometimes we come up against a circumstance or an event that just makes us want to give up and stop. What we do when that happens will greatly affect our success in our life's race.

My mother,
Emma Martin Schwartz.

When my mother, Emma Martin, was in her teens, she hit an unanticipated wall. Her mother—my Grandmother Martin—suffered a series of strokes that left her paralyzed and unable to speak. My mother assumed her mother's role of cooking, cleaning, and caring for her father and her three brothers, along with attending school. She also cared lovingly for her mother each day.

This situation must have been very difficult, and the additional responsibilities she had to assume at such an early age must have been hard to bear. But I am told that my mother never complained and was patient and kind to her mother, father, and brothers. She did not let her circumstances discourage her or excuse her from achieving her goals and dreams. In fact, she continued to attend school and gain further education. When she graduated from high school, she was given an award for never having missed a day of school in twelve years. She had also earned the highest grades possible in all her classes.

After her graduation, my mother attended college in a city several miles away. Each weekend she would return home to care for her mother. She would change the beds, do the washing, clean the house, and prepare meals for the week for her family, and then return to school on Monday morning. When she met and married my father, they moved into her parents' home so that she could continue to care for her parents. I was raised in that home and still carry with me the memories of my mother's service and sacrifice. My life has been richly blessed because of her example.

Because of my mother's attitude, I always thought it was a privilege to live with my grandparents. I came to know them in a way I could never have otherwise. I loved my Grandmother Martin dearly, and even though she could not speak, I knew she loved me by the look in her eyes. I learned how to read on her lap. She was always there and was never too busy to listen to me. Her attitude was one of cheer and optimism. She was grateful for the smallest things. She loved it when I helped her walk around the living room, and she loved to go for a ride in the car. She blessed my life as a young child and as an adult.

Both my mother and my grandmother were talented, educated, capable women. I am sure this was not what my grandmother had envisioned for her life, nor was it what my mother had in mind for her life.

Life's journey sometimes takes us on unexpected paths. There are twists and turns in the road that none of us can anticipate. But with each of these twists and turns there is also opportunity—opportunity to choose our response and our plan of action. Difficulties in life can be insurmountable walls—or they can be opportunities to help us draw closer to the Savior and to trust in Him more fully. In the process of living close to Him each day, we develop Christlike attributes and qualities.

For me, my mother and grandmother are modern-day

examples of the virtues and qualities that women in earlier dispensations developed as they exercised their dedication to the Lord.

As I study the scriptures and Church history, I am reminded again and again that the lives of many great people—in fact, the lives of most—did not go as they might have planned. How they saw their lives and how the Lord saw their lives were sometimes entirely different. In some cases He even sent angels to provide course corrections (see Mosiah 27:11–17).

In 1856, at age thirteen, Mary Goble joined the Church with her family in England, traveled to America, and joined the Martin Handcart Company. In her personal history she recounts the difficulty of the journey—the loss of her baby brother and older brother, the freezing of her own feet, and finally the death of an infant sister and her mother. When she arrived in the Salt Lake Valley, the doctor amputated her toes, but she was promised by the prophet, Brigham Young, that she would not have to have any more of her feet cut off. She recounts: "One day I sat there crying. My feet were hurting me so—when a little old woman knocked at the door. She said she had felt someone needed her there for a number of days. . . . I showed her my feet and told her the promise Bro. Young had given me. She said, 'Yes, and with the help of the Lord we will save them yet.' She made a poultice and put on my feet and every day after the doctor had gone she would come and change the poultice. At the end of three months my feet were well" (in Cracroft and Lambert, *A Believing People*, 145).

Although her feet had healed, Mary had sat in her chair for so long that the muscles in her legs had become stiff, and she could not straighten her legs. Her condition brought both Mary and her father to tears. They tried rubbing oil on her legs and doing anything they could think of to help straighten them. But nothing worked. Then, Mary recounted, "One day [Father] said, 'Mary, I have thought of a plan to help you. I will nail a shelf on the wall and while I am away to work you try to reach it.' I tried all day, and for several days. At last I could reach it and how pleased we were. Then [Father] put the shelf a little higher and in about three months my legs were straight and then I had to learn to walk again" (in Cracroft and Lambert, *A Believing People,* 145).

Certainly Mary Goble hit a wall of serious proportions, but little by little, with diligent effort and a will to keep moving, she was able to move forward again.

I see this theme repeated in the lives of many righteous women in the scriptures. Ruth and Hannah are two scriptural women whose lives took an unexpected direction. Ruth did not expect that her husband would die, and Hannah did not expect to be unable to bear children after she was married. Each of us can be tutored as we study their lives and their reactions to the situations that presented themselves. Like my mother and grandmother and Mary Goble, they possessed faith, hope, and charity, which enabled them to face their trials and to be instruments in the Lord's hands for achieving His purposes.

FAITH

Both Ruth and Hannah had great faith. The Prophet Joseph Smith taught that faith is "the first principle in revealed religion, and the foundation of all righteousness" (*Lectures on Faith,* "Lecture First," paragraph 1). And we are told in Hebrews 11 that "faith is the substance of things hoped for, the evidence of things not seen" (v. 1). These righteous and faithful women could not see what the future held; yet they were faithful to the Lord and to the covenants they had made.

After the death of her husband, Ruth chose to remain with her mother-in-law, Naomi. In making this decision, she gave up her family's Moabite traditions in favor of the truths of the God of Israel.

The choice to forsake family, friends, or other familiar circumstances is a difficult choice that new converts and others sometimes make because they have gained a testimony of the truths of the restored gospel and have put their trust in the Lord. Like Ruth, they exercise great faith as they make changes to align their lives to the new truths they have been taught.

Several years ago, I became acquainted with a young woman from India. She was visiting the United States and was staying in the home of a wonderful Latter-day Saint family. They taught her the gospel by the way they lived. She observed their great faith and love of the Lord and how it affected everything they did. She joined in family home evening lessons and activities every Monday night. She began to read the Book of Mormon and to attend church. She was taught the gospel and gained a testimony of its truthfulness, and she was baptized. When she joined the Church, she was in a sense doing what Ruth had done. It took courage to tell her parents and family, but she knew the Church was true and she had such great faith that she was willing to give up everything to have the blessings of the gospel in her life. She is a latter-day Ruth.

Hannah is a powerful example of faithfulness. Her petition to be blessed with a child was granted after the trial of her faith. She covenanted with the Lord that she would give her son to His service when her son was old enough, and she remained committed to her covenant. Her words reveal the depth of her faithful commitment: "For this child I prayed; and the Lord hath given me my petition which I asked of him: Therefore also I have lent him to the Lord; as long as he liveth he shall be lent to the Lord" (1 Samuel 1:27–28).

It is interesting to note that Hannah's story begins with a cry of distress and sorrow to the Lord and ends with a song of praise and thanksgiving to the Lord. We do not always have the option of choosing our situations in life, but we can respond with faith and trust in the Savior. We can know that He knows and loves us and will be with us. He has promised in the Doctrine and Covenants: "Ye cannot bear all things now; nevertheless, be of good cheer, for I will lead you along. The kingdom is yours and the blessings thereof are yours, and the riches of eternity are yours" (78:18). We can also know that when we exercise our faith, the Lord's purposes will be accomplished in His own way and in His own timing, and in the end, everything will work for our good. We can play a part in blessing future generations by exercising our faith in the Lord as we move forward through trials.

HOPE

Hannah and Ruth possessed not only great faith but also hope. We learn from Mormon, as recorded in Moroni, that "if a man have faith he must needs have hope; for without faith there cannot be any hope" (Moroni 7:42). When the life circumstances of these women were changed—when they hit the wall, so to speak—they had hope that the Lord would provide guidance and strength.

Hannah, unable to have children, turned to the Lord in the temple and "poured out [her] soul before" Him (1 Samuel 1:15). Hannah was disappointed that her righteous desires had not been granted. However, she loved the Lord and had hope and trust in His might.

Ruth looked to the Lord with hope for her future. When she lost her husband, she experienced the feelings of loneliness that her mother-in-law, Naomi, had borne when her own husband had died. Ruth's compassion and faithfulness to Naomi are demonstrated in some of the most beautiful words ever uttered: "Intreat me not to leave thee, or to return from following after thee: for whither thou goest, I will go; and where thou lodgest, I will lodge: thy people shall be my people, and thy God my God" (Ruth 1:16).

Ruth loved the Lord, and her faith and hope in Him were strong. Neither she nor Hannah gave up their hope. Rather, it sustained them in their trials.

CHARITY

These two women possessed not only the qualities of faith and hope but also those of devotion and sacrifice. These Christlike qualities are among the fruits of charity. Hannah and Ruth loved the Lord, and they loved His children. They were willing to put their own desires and futures aside to do what was right. Each of these women made a commitment to the Lord based on her faith and her hope in His goodness and mercy.

Although Hannah consecrated her son, Samuel, to the Lord, she continued to demonstrate great love and dedication to him, as shown by her yearly visits to the temple: "His mother made him a little coat, and brought it to him from year to year, when she came up with her husband to offer the yearly sacrifice" (1 Samuel 2:19).

In a small way, mothers all over the world feel what Hannah must have felt as they prepare their sons and daughters to serve missions. Hannah's love of the Lord and love of her son are also poignant reminders of God's love for His children.

Similarly, because of Ruth's unselfish love and obedience to Naomi, she eventually married Boaz and had a child named Obed. Through her lineage, the Savior was born.

"A FULL REWARD BE GIVEN THEE"

Like Ruth and Hannah, all of us will experience adversity. We may not always understand the Lord's design for our lives, but it is my testimony that we are never alone. He is ever with us, and He promises us, "Ye cannot behold with your natural eyes, for the present time, the design of your God concerning those things which shall come hereafter, and the glory which shall follow after much tribulation" (Doctrine and Covenants 58:3).

I am grateful for the pattern of faith, hope, and charity that is shown to me in the lives of righteous women in the scriptures. I am also grateful for my mother, who trusted in the Lord and leaned not unto her own understanding (see Proverbs 3:5). I believe that what was said to Ruth could be said of my mother and grandmother and the many others who navigate life's challenges with faith and trust in the Lord: "The Lord recompense thy work, and a full reward be given thee of the Lord . . . under whose wings thou art come to trust" (Ruth 2:12).

Chapter 6

Staying on Course

Repenting and Returning to Virtue

On one of the trails in a canyon near my home, there is a sign that says "Stay on the Path." As one embarks on that trail, it soon becomes very clear that this is sound advice. There are hills and turns and steep drop-off areas. In some places the ground beyond the path is unstable, and during certain seasons of the year, an occasional rattlesnake appears.

For anyone running a race, that advice is good. Stay on the path. It is the surest way to keep safe and to cross the finish line successfully.

Several years ago I went on a backpacking trip in the Teton Mountains of Wyoming with a group of young women. It was a difficult hike, and on the second day we arrived at the most dangerous part of the hike. We were going to hike along Hurricane Pass—aptly named because of the strong winds which almost always blow there. We were instructed by a ranger to stay in the center of the path, stay as low as possible on the exposed part of the trail, secure everything in our packs, and move quickly. This was no spot for taking photographs or for lingering. I was very relieved and happy when each one of the young women had

Celebrating a safe passage through Hurricane Pass
(left to right:) Leslie Robbins, Elaine Dalton,
Emi Dalton Edgley, Linda Dunn

navigated that spot successfully. And do you know—not one of them asked how close to the edge they could get!

Sometimes, as we walk life's paths, we want to loiter in dangerous places, thinking that it is fun and thrilling and that we are in control. Sometimes we think we can live on the edge and still maintain our virtue. But that is a risky place to be. As the Prophet Joseph Smith told us, "Happiness is the object and design of our existence; and will be the end thereof, if we pursue the path that leads to it; and this path is virtue" (*History of the Church*, 5:134–35).

We are counseled in Doctrine and Covenants section 25 that we must *cleave* to our covenants (see v. 13). *Cleaving*, to me, means to stick to, to adhere, and to really hold on tight to the promises we make with the Lord. Our covenants will strengthen us to resist temptation. Keeping our covenants will steady us on the path of virtue. As we keep the covenants we have made at baptism, we will remain in the center of the path.

Elder Jeffrey R. Holland reminds us: "Beginning with our baptism, we make covenants as we follow this path to eternal life, and we stay on the path by keeping them. . . . The promptings of the Holy Ghost will always be sufficient for our needs if we keep to the covenant path. Our path is uphill most days, but the help we receive for the climb is literally divine. We have three members of the Godhead—the Father, the Son, and the Holy Ghost—helping us because of the covenants we have made" ("What I Wish Every Member Knew," 11–12).

The Book of Mormon describes what happened when a whole society kept their covenants and lived clean and virtuous lives: "And surely there could not be a happier people among all the people who had been created by the hand of God" (4 Nephi 1:16).

I have in my office the pictures of the generations of women in my family—my great-grandmother, my grandmother, my mother, and my daughter, Emi. Their lives of commitment and faith in the plan have helped me climb higher and journey further. Looking at that picture now, I can see very clearly the importance of living a virtuous life. Today I not only have one daughter, but five daughters-in-law and eleven little granddaughters to add to that picture. I feel a deep sense of responsibility to live an exemplary life of virtue and holiness before them. Even if you are the first in the line of generations to come, you too have a responsibility to those that will follow you. Guided by the Holy Ghost, you will also be a righteous influence on others.

Recently, I embarked on that same hike in the Tetons I mentioned earlier, only this time with my husband and a group of friends our same age. When we started, it was thrilling and easy, but before we arrived at our destination, we were exhausted and

I knew I was in trouble. I was not as prepared for the hike physically as I had been when I hiked with the young women years before—and I had packed my equipment carelessly and taken too much. The weight of my pack began to make me weary and ready to give up. The others were also feeling the rigors of the altitude, the steep terrain, and heavy packs. My husband sensed this and hurried ahead. I felt abandoned. However, after about an hour I could see my husband descending the trail on the other side of the valley. He was running toward me. When he reached me, he took my pack, dried my tears, and led me to the destination—a crystal clear lake surrounded by lofty pine trees. Then he turned around, went back down the trail, and did the same thing four more times for the other hikers. As I watched him, I was sorry I was so unprepared and even more sorry that I had so many extra things in my pack that had added to the weight he had to carry for me. But I was so grateful for his strength, for his unselfishness, for his preparation, and for his love.

As you climb the mountains of life, stay on the path of virtue. There will be others to help you—your parents, family members, bishops, advisers, and righteous friends of all ages. And if you are weary or take a wrong turn, change your direction and get back on the path of virtue. Always remember that the Savior is there for you. He will enable you to repent, strengthen you, lighten your burdens, dry your tears, comfort you, and continue to help you stay on the path.

Once, after I had given a talk on the Christlike attribute of virtue to a mixed audience of youth, young adults, and families, a young woman approached me afterwards and said, "Sister

Dalton, you talk of virtue, but don't you realize that being virtuous is not possible or realistic in today's world?" As I looked into her eyes, I saw her sincerity and also her pain. In response to her question, I asked another: "Do you believe in Jesus Christ?" When she responded that she did, I shared my testimony that because of Him, it *is* possible to be virtuous. And if one has not been virtuous, because of Him it is possible to return to virtue. I explained that the Savior has shown us the way by setting a perfect example for us to follow. And He has given each of us the invitation to follow His example and to become like Him. He came to the earth to make it possible for each one of us to return to live with God again. When we make a mistake, it is possible to repent because of His infinite Atonement. And although repentance is not easy, it is possible because of Him. I suggested that she begin reading the Book of Mormon and note what the Redeemer and those who followed Him did to live virtuous lives. I asked her to liken the scriptures to her life and circumstances. I told her that I felt that as we learn of Him and incorporate His attributes into our lives, we can be an influence for good in the world. I then shared with her that I believe that one virtuous young woman or young man, led by the Spirit, can change the world.

For example, a young man I know well was elected to be the student body president at a large university. The university sent him to a leadership seminar where student leaders from across the United States gathered in Chicago, Illinois, to be trained and educated. They participated in an initial game outdoors on the college campus so that they could become acquainted with each other. The students were presented with current issues facing to-day's youth and were asked to take a position. In response to the issue presented, they were directed to run to several trees in the grassy area marked "strongly agree," "partially agree," "strongly disagree," or "mildly disagree."

Toward the end of this exercise, the leader asked, "Do you believe in premarital sex?" Without hesitation, this young man ran to the tree marked "strongly disagree." To his amazement, he was the only one there! All the other student leaders were laughing and pointing at him and saying, "Oh, Jess, you are so funny. We all know you're not really serious." At that moment Jess said he knew exactly what he must do and so he loudly declared, "I'm not funny. I'm serious!" There was a stunned silence, and then the group dispersed, leaving Jess standing alone by the tree. He felt out of place and yes, weird. But he wasn't weird. He was right. And he was not alone. During the week, many of the student leaders came to him privately and said that they wished they had known years earlier what he knew. Jess later said, "It was easy because I knew that I represented not only the university but my family, the Church, and the Savior."

Is it possible to stay on the path of virtue in today's world, even considering all that we are faced with? I testify that it is.

Without virtue, there can be no purity, and without purity, there can be no companionship of a member of the Godhead— the Holy Ghost. We know that virtue is a prerequisite to receiving the Spirit's guidance, since "the Holy Ghost does not dwell in unclean tabernacles" (*Preach My Gospel,* 118). Without the Spirit's guidance, faith would soon languish and die. Faith in the Lord

Jesus Christ, strengthened through virtuous living and behavior, leads to inspired knowledge and increased spirituality (see 2 Peter 1:8). Is it any wonder that Peter admonished the early Saints to "add to [their] faith virtue; and to virtue knowledge" (2 Peter 1:5)? Without a call to the world for a return to virtue, the loss of our youth and the disintegration of the eternal family in today's world will be staggering. For truly we are still engaged in a war that began in the premortal existence and has merely changed venues.

I need not remind any of you of the statistics regarding immorality, disease, abortion, or divorce. Prophets have long foretold that among the most serious challenges to the Church in the latter days would be sexual immorality. President Joseph F. Smith said that three tests would come upon the Church from within, the most vital of which would be maintaining sexual purity. He said, "If purity of life is neglected, all other dangers set in upon us like the rivers of waters when the flood gates are opened" (*Gospel Doctrine*, 313). President Ezra Taft Benson asked, "Why is it we rarely hear anyone calling for a return to chastity, for a commitment to virtue and fidelity?" ("The Law of Chastity," 4). We are all aware of the well-planned, well-funded campaign the adversary is waging, using the rich and famous and twisting tools that could be used to achieve great good, corrupting them for his evil purposes. And so the Lord admonishes us in these latter days to "say nothing but repentance unto this generation" (Doctrine and Covenants 6:9).

Let me share with you an experience I had shortly after I was called to be the Young Women general president. As a presidency

we visited a group of young women who were in a drug rehabili-
tation center. Our purpose was to minister, to lift, to love, and to
learn. Around the table were seated twelve of the most beautiful
young women I had ever seen. Their eyes told their stories without words. I began: "What got you here? Was this in your plan?"
They smiled and laughed and then they began to respond. Each
shared that she had no idea that the things she was doing would
eventually culminate in this place. One young woman thought
her parents were too strict, and so one night she became angry
and sneaked out her window to go with her friends. That's where
it all began—with anger. Another young woman was hurting because of an uncle who had caused her harm, and she had lost her
sense of worth and tried to mask the hurt with drugs. Another
young woman said it started with small indiscretions and a little
voice inside that said, "You are bad. You don't belong at Church.
You don't fit in. You can't pray." Another confessed that she didn't
know she could repent. She thought that because of her mistake,
all was lost and she could not change.

We then asked what made the difference and what was
helping them to progress. One young woman said that she saw
a picture of Jesus one night in one of the rooms. The children
were surrounding Him, and His face looked so compassionate.
She had the feeling that she should pray. She said it was hard to
kneel and begin, but that once she did, a feeling she could not
describe enveloped her and when she finished her prayer, everything changed. "That is when I received the strength to change,"
she said. We asked what we should tell other young women to
help them. They said, "Tell them that their parents are really right

and that they do things out of love. Tell them that family really is the most important thing and that your parents really are some of your best friends. Tell them not to listen to voices that say you are bad. Tell them to pray always. And tell them they can repent— they can change. We didn't know that."

President Henry B. Eyring taught that the Greek word translated as *repentance* means "to have a new mind" (*To Draw Closer to God*, 47). Repentance means to turn away or turn around. It means to change. Repentance is not merely following a five-step process or simply the cessation of doing wrong, nor the expression of sorrow or the passage of time. Although these are each part of the process, none of them alone is true repentance. As those young women knew only too well, true repentance requires great effort to change. Alma the Younger described true repentance when he told the people of Zarahemla of the life of his father, Alma the Elder, who had heard Abinadi's testimony of the Atonement of the Savior in wicked King Noah's court. There, he had been changed. That prophetic testimony penetrated his heart and, Alma the Younger observed, "According to his faith there was a mighty change wrought in his heart" (Alma 5:12). That is true repentance.

RETURN AND REPENT

Ever since our Young Women general presidency began calling for a "return to virtue" to the world, many youth have come up to us after firesides and other meetings with tears in their eyes. They say, "Does that mean I can return?" So many times

77

in scripture the Savior calls for us to "return." When He visited the New World, He questioned, "O all ye that are spared because ye were more righteous than they, will ye not now *return* unto me, and repent of your sins, and be converted, that I may heal you?" (3 Nephi 9:13; emphasis added). "Even from the days of your fathers ye are gone away from mine ordinances, and have not kept them. *Return* unto me and I will *return* unto you, saith the Lord of Hosts" (3 Nephi 24:7; emphasis added). The ancient prophet Amos described all the things the Lord did to help the people return and repent, including rain and pestilence and famine, and yet he lamented, "Have ye not *returned* unto me" (Amos 4:9). In spite of it all, they did not return unto the Lord. Jeremiah described the generation of his day in terms that sound familiar today: "Were they ashamed when they had committed abomination? nay, they were not at all ashamed, neither could they blush" (Jeremiah 6:15; 8:12). Is our generation becoming an "unblushable" one? When King Benjamin finished his remarkable address in the land of Zarahemla, the people all cried with one voice that they believed his words. They knew of a surety that his promises of redemption were true, because, they said, "the Spirit of the Lord Omnipotent . . . has wrought a mighty change in us, or in our hearts, [and note this] that we have no more disposition to do evil, but to do good continually" (Mosiah 5:2). What is it really that creates this mighty change of heart? It is the Spirit! And what brings the Spirit? Repentance!

Blessings Await Us

As we repent and return to virtue, our Father in Heaven stands ready to bless us so abundantly. For those who stay on the path or those who repent and return, the promises are sure.

The blessings of obedience are illustrated in the story of a young man from Singapore, who e-mailed me after I had given a talk in which I had mentioned a marathon my husband and I had run. He wanted to know if I thought it was all right to run a marathon on a Sunday. He explained that he was an avid runner and an active member of the Church and that he was training for the Singapore Marathon, which was held on a Sunday. He said that he did not have a lot of money and he did not think he would ever be able to run a marathon anywhere else where a marathon might possibly be held on another day of the week. He felt this was his only opportunity to participate in a marathon experience. He said he thought this exception might be acceptable given his special circumstances. He wanted me to advise him as to what he should do. I responded with the following reply:

"Dear Brother Lai, I cannot make that decision for you. You will need to be prayerful and decide for yourself. But I have always turned to the scripture in 1 Samuel, chapter 2, verse 30 to help me with decisions. Perhaps it will also help you."

I quoted the scripture and ended my letter. The scripture reads in part: "but now the Lord saith . . . for them that honour me I will honour" (1 Samuel 2:30). I never heard anything else from this good brother, and I wondered what his decision had been on the date of the Singapore Marathon.

Two years later, I was assigned to do some auxiliary training in the Asia area. One of the places where I would train was Singapore. I was curious to see this beautiful city. When I arrived at the Singapore airport, there waiting to greet me were the area presidency member assigned to accompany us and Brother Lai, the man who had written me about running on Sunday. I was thrilled to meet him. You can probably guess that the first question I asked him was, "Did you run the marathon?" He responded eagerly that he had! I smiled and said, "Congratulations!" But in my heart I was sad—it seemed like I hadn't quite gotten my point across, and I regretted not being more direct in my reply. Then he added quietly, "But I did rather poorly. I ran it all alone on Saturday in the traffic." And the scripture went through my mind once again, reminding me that he who honors God, God will honor. Stephen Lai had been faithful and obedient.

One year later, I received a phone call from Singapore. Brother Lai was coming to Salt Lake for business. He said he thought it was a true miracle because the timing of the trip was such that he would be able to attend general conference, take care of his business obligation, and the next Saturday participate in the St. George Marathon. He wanted to know if he could go with our family to conference and then to the marathon. He was so excited and kept talking about the miracle of it all.

The week after general conference we traveled to St. George, Utah, where we all participated in this marathon. When I crossed the finish line, Brother Lai was there to cheer me on. He was so happy, all I could see was a big smile. Later he told my husband that when he crossed the finish line, the words of the scripture I had sent him went through his mind, a warmth surged through his body, and he knew that he had done the right thing. He said, "Had I run the Singapore Marathon, it would have been a little thing. No one would have known. But I exercised my faith, and because I was obedient, I have been blessed beyond my dreams. I am here, I have been in the presence of a prophet of God, and I am worthy to be in his presence—no excuses or apologies."

Stephen Lai honored God by keeping the Sabbath day holy. He did not rationalize by saying that commandment didn't apply to him in his individual and unique circumstances. He did not assume he was the exception. We too can honor the Lord through our obedience to Him.

When you obey the commandments of the Lord, you will always be blessed. Stay on the path. If you have stepped off, for whatever reason, repent and return to Him, and all those blessings can still be yours. Sometimes the blessings are not immediate, but you are always blessed—always—when you are striving to live a virtuous life.

Chapter 7

THE FINISH LINE

Virtue and the Temple

Imagine a race without a finish line! Fortunately, for us the goal is clear. The culmination of our race for virtue is the temple—whether it be your first time entering His holy house, or one of the many times you faithfully return throughout your life. Receiving the blessings of the temple—and continuing to qualify for them by keeping the covenants made therein—is one of the crowning achievements and purposes of this mortal life.

When I was a young girl, my grandfather used to tell me about the temple. He said that the day would come when temples would literally dot the earth. I could hardly imagine what that meant. Brigham Young said, "To accomplish this work there will have to be not only one temple but thousands of them, and thousands and tens of thousands of men and women will go into those temples and officiate for people who have lived as far back as the Lord shall reveal" (*Discourses of Brigham Young,* 394). Have you ever wondered what you did or who you were in the premortal realms to deserve the honor, privilege, and sacred trust to be on the earth now—living in this, the dispensation of the fullness of times, as these events are coming to pass?

When our children were young and my husband was away from home serving in the bishopric, and gas was cheap, I used to load the children into our little brown Pinto and take them for what we fondly referred to as "night rides." I was desperate! It was my attempt to settle the children and make them sleepy enough to go to bed when we returned home. We would drive to downtown Salt Lake City and circle Temple Square. As the children looked toward the temple, we talked about the temple spires, the granite blocks carved by pioneers, and the angel Moroni. I would tell the children about the day that their father and I were married in the temple. They never tired of this ritual or this story even though it was always the same. In fact, they corrected me when I would forget a detail of the account! As we drove toward home, I would ask the children, "Where are you going to get married?" Our little Emi would reply with her two-year-old enthusiasm, "The nemple, the nemple!" How eternally significant have been the days when each of our six children have gone to the "nemple" to be married. It seemed just a blink away since those "night rides" of their youth.

I now believe that those night rides taken by a young, desperate mother were a great blessing in our life because as we circled the temple, the temple encircled our children. Looking toward the temple also blessed and strengthened me. I found that the words inscribed on the east side become emblazoned on my heart: "Holiness to the Lord. The House of the Lord."

What does "Holiness to the Lord" mean? I believe it means purity, righteousness, and sanctification. In 2 Nephi 9:20, the first footnote uses the word *committed* to define *holiness* in that context. When we are holy before the Lord, we are pure and worthy. We are *committed* to Him through our covenants. We are committed to His plan of happiness, to His ways, to His standards. Our commitments didn't start at the temple; they began in the premortal realms, where each one of us made a commitment to our Heavenly Father, and to His Son, and to the plan that was proposed by the Father.

Our pioneer ancestors knew it was all about the temple. That is one of the reasons the Relief Society was organized—so that the women could assist in the work of the temple. They made shirts for the men as they worked to build the Nauvoo Temple. They provided meals. They provided relief so that in their poverty a temple could be built. They knew that success in mortality wasn't about possessions, but about power and strength derived from eternal covenants and eternal ordinances. They knew that they were on a journey back to their heavenly home. They glimpsed eternity. On the walls of the Nauvoo Temple they inscribed in gold: "The Lord has seen our sacrifice, come after us." They intended those words for us.

I am so grateful to those noble Saints, our ancestors, for their vision, their faith, their sacrifice, and their example. To them I would say, "We have seen your sacrifice. It is not in vain. We will come after you!"

As temples now dot the earth, their presence is felt. How do we commit ourselves and our lives in such a way that we qualify for the blessings of the temple? What can we do to put aside the things of the world and seek for the things of a better world?

To begin with, we must understand our identity. In the Book of Mormon we are described in this way: "Ye are the children of the prophets; and ye are of the house of Israel; and ye are of the covenant which the Father made with your fathers" (3 Nephi 20:25). Elder Russell M. Nelson said, "Once we know who we are, and the royal lineage of which we are a part, our actions and our direction in life will be more appropriate to our inheritance" (*Perfection Pending*, 208). When we truly know that we are children of God and have an understanding of our divine nature, it will be reflected in our countenance, our appearance, our actions, and our priorities.

Alma tells us that we were "called and prepared from the foundation of the world according to the foreknowledge of God, on account of [our] exceeding faith and good works" (Alma 13:3). Not just faith, but *exceeding* faith and good works! We had faith in the Savior, in the Father, and in the plan that was presented, and we are here now to do that which we said we would do then. It is a divine compliment that you and I are on the earth now, in the dispensation of the fullness of times. Today we have the gospel that has been restored to the earth. We have prophets and priesthood power. We have the Book of Mormon. We have holy temples where we can make covenants that will protect and direct us, as we have experiences that refine and make us pure to again return to the presence of God and His beloved Son. We have a great work to do.

Satan will not only try to discredit the work we are here to do in temples but also distract us from that work. We may become too busy, or we may think that since all is not perfect in our homes or relationships, we should not go. There may be voices that tell us to wait, that surely if a son or daughter is not doing

what is right, that we as their parents are failures and not worthy of temple blessings. These are false and deceiving voices. We simply cannot listen to them when they speak. It is time to "run to the temple!"

CLEAVING TO OUR COVENANTS

We must be virtuous and pure in order to enter into the Lord's holy temples and do the work we have been prepared and reserved to do. The Lord has said that "no unclean thing shall be allowed to come into thy house to pollute it" (Doctrine and Covenants 109:20). Satan knows this, and he has launched his attack to disqualify and distract each of us from the work to be done in temples. We must firmly set our hearts on those things that matter most. We cannot allow ourselves to become distracted, distraught, or discouraged. Think of the transformation that could occur in the world through the righteous influence of each committed Latter-day Saint. What would happen if each of us simply determined not to be lured away from those things that matter most? Our righteous influence and actions can and will change the world.

The Lord has made it clear that He desires to have a pure and virtuous people. The temple provides the perfect pattern for such refinement. It is no accident that the symbolic color of the Young Woman value of virtue is gold. Gold is pure and soft, and it shines because it has been refined. When gold is refined, it is put under intense heat and melted into a liquid state, and then a material called flux is added. Flux causes the impurities to part from the gold. It is a refining process. The interesting thing about flux is that it has to be pure in order for this process to work.

There is meaning in this process for our lives. We become refined as we prepare for and go to the temple. It is within these hallowed walls that we may "receive a fulness of the Holy Ghost" (Doctrine and Covenants 109:15). Receiving the Holy Ghost purifies and refines us as if with fire. When we enter the temple, we make a physical parting from the world. Our actions, our dress, and our language, not to mention our priorities, are different—they are refined. Every ordinance and covenant binds us to the Savior. It is through His example and pure and perfect life that we are strengthened and enabled. It is because of His infinite Atonement that we can repent and become pure and virtuous. *He* is the pure addition we need to be enabled to enter into the Father's presence once again. His Atonement is the basis for every temple ordinance. Every ordinance and covenant we make refines us and binds us to the Savior.

Our temple covenants set us apart from the people of the world. A covenant is a binding agreement between man and God. When we keep our covenants, the Lord has promised us spiritual blessings. Our covenants not only define us, they *refine* us.

The counsel of the Lord to Emma Smith—and it is His counsel to *all* his precious daughters—was to "walk in the paths of virtue before me" and to "cleave unto the covenants which thou hast made" (Doctrine and Covenants 25:2, 13). When we are virtuous and cleave to our covenants, we are blessed. A covenant made with God is not burdensome or restrictive; it is protective

and enabling. Personal worthiness is essential to enter His holy temples and to ultimately become heirs to "all that [the] Father hath" (Doctrine and Covenants 84:38).

Why did the Lord tell us to "cleave to our covenants"? It is because making and keeping covenants will help us be worthy to hear and receive promptings from the Holy Ghost. It is because of the "protecting power of the ordinances and covenants available in the house of the Lord" (Bednar, "Honorably Hold a Name and Standing," 99). If we want that protection from the adversary, it can be found as we keep our covenants.

The sacrament we partake of each week helps us renew our covenants, and it is there that we covenant to "be willing" to take His name upon us. Elder Bednar taught: "The baptismal covenant clearly contemplates a future event or events and looks forward to the temple. . . . The process of taking upon ourselves the name of Jesus Christ that is commenced in the waters of baptism is continued and enlarged in the house of the Lord. As we stand in the waters of baptism, we look to the temple. As we partake of the sacrament, we look to the temple. We pledge to always remember the Savior and to keep His commandments as preparation to participate in the sacred ordinances of the temple and receive the highest blessings available through the name and by the authority of the Lord Jesus Christ. Thus, in the ordinances of the holy temple we more completely and fully take upon us the name of Jesus Christ" ("Honorably Hold a Name and Standing," 98).

I resonate with the scripture in Doctrine and Covenants section 109 in which "a testimony of the covenant" is invoked on all who attend the temple worthily (v. 38). I bear my testimony of these sacred covenants and the power that comes into our lives as a result.

The Salt Lake Temple baptistry is a thrilling place to be on Saturday mornings! I was there early one morning to be baptized for some of my ancestors. As I sat waiting on the bench in the baptismal area, I noticed that the young woman on my left was reading her patriarchal blessing. The girl on my right was reading her scriptures. I asked her if she had come here with a group. Her reply was: "No, I come with my friend every Saturday. It makes my whole week go better." These young women, along with many other young men and women, know a grand secret—the temple blesses not only our families' and ancestors' lives, but also our own. We are promised that those who are endowed in the temple will go forth from that holy house "armed with thy power, and that thy name may be upon them, and thy glory be round about them, and thine angels have charge over them" (Doctrine and Covenants 109:22). These are great blessings and promises. Who would not desire to prepare to receive these blessings in order to navigate in today's ever-darkening world?

Recently I was traveling in a large city in South America on an assignment. When we arrived it was dark and the traffic was heavy, making it difficult to navigate and find the correct direction of the mission home where we were to stay. Then the driver said, "I can find the way. It is easy. I just look toward the temple." Far off in the distance I could see the lights on the spires of the temple and angel Moroni.

Similarly, as we keep our eyes on the temple and navigate by that light, we will be able to keep our sense of direction. We will not wander, and we will be enabled to stay on the path that leads to eternal life. Daily decisions will be clear if we look toward the temple. Recently, I asked a young woman how she stays pure and virtuous when surrounded daily by the darkness of foul language, sights, and sounds. Holding her Young Women medallion, which has the image of the temple on it, she replied, "I wear *this* every single day. When I touch it, it helps me stay focused on the temple and remain pure, virtuous, and worthy to enter there." This young woman was looking toward the temple.

The Lord has said, "Let virtue garnish thy thoughts unceasingly; then shall thy confidence wax strong in the presence of God" (Doctrine and Covenants 121:45). When we do this, we can confidently enter the holy temples of God with a knowledge that we are worthy to go where the Lord Himself goes. When we are worthy, we can not only *enter* the temple, the temple can *enter* us. The Lord's promises of salvation and happiness become *ours*—and our earthly mission becomes *His.*

A young woman's treasured medallion

LOOKING TOWARD ETERNITY

When our youngest son, Chad, was married, our entire family was together in a sealing room of the Salt Lake Temple. The mirrors I had looked into when I was married appeared different to me that day because when I looked into them, I saw not only my reflection and my husband's reflection go on and on, but also the reflections of all my children and their spouses. They went on and on as far as I could see. In that moment, I understood anew the importance of looking toward the temple, remaining pure and virtuous, and making and keeping sacred covenants.

I was reminded of the day years before when our first grandson, Isaac, was born. The entire family rushed to the hospital. It was an amazing experience for me to see our oldest son, Matthew, holding this precious new baby boy. While standing at the nursery window with our youngest son, Chad, we gazed into the eyes of this new little spirit—so clean, so pure, so recently from heaven. It seemed that all time stood still, and for an instant, we could see the great eternal plan. The sacredness of life was crystal clear, and I whispered to Chad, "Do you understand why it is so important to remain clean and pure?" He responded reverently, "Oh yes, Mom, I get it."

Now, as Chad took the hand of his beautiful bride and knelt with her at the altar of the temple, I looked into the mirrors on either side and again I wanted to whisper, "Do you understand why it is so important to be clean and pure?" But this time I didn't have to remind him because the Spirit did the whispering.

In the temple we learn everything we need to know and do to return back into the presence of our Heavenly Father and His Son Jesus Christ. Every ordinance helps us understand the redeeming and enabling power of the Savior's Atonement. Moroni understood this: "Yea, come unto Christ and be perfected in Him" (Moroni 10:32).

At the end of the Book of Mormon, Moroni issued the final ultimate appeal to each of us to be virtuous and pure and to keep our covenants. "Come unto Christ, and lay hold upon every good gift, and touch not the evil gift nor the unclean thing. . . . Awake, and arise from the dust . . . yea, and put on thy beautiful garments, O daughter of Zion; . . . that the covenants of the Eternal Father which he hath made unto thee . . . may be fulfilled" (Moroni 10:30–31).

My prayer is the same as Moroni's—that we, the sons and daughters of Zion, may "come unto Christ and be perfected in Him" (Moroni 10:32). That when He shall appear, we will be like Him—pure even as He is pure. I know that as we understand our identity and place in this matchless plan, and as we continue to look toward the temple, our lives of virtue and covenant will bless generations.

Chapter 8

COACHING OTHERS

Raising Up a Virtuous Generation

Once our experiences have taught us some useful lessons about running the marathon of life, our natural inclination is to want to pass those lessons on to the next generation. We become the "coaches," helping train future marathoners to run their own races well.

As those who are "primarily responsible for the nurture of their children" ("The Family: A Proclamation," paragraph 7), mothers are particularly important coaches. I think it is so important that we talk about and exemplify the privilege it is to be women on the earth at this time and to have been given the divine trust to be mothers of other eternal souls. I can think of no greater position we could occupy and no greater honor we could have. We have been entrusted with the nurture and tutoring of God's precious children.

When I was first called to serve as the second counselor in the general Young Women presidency, our presidency had a meeting with President Gordon B. Hinckley. We told him of our hopes and dreams for young women all over the world. We said that we wanted them to know their identity—that they are daughters of God. We said that we wanted them to know that they can receive strength and be guided as they rely on prayer and the Holy Ghost, and we told him that we wanted them to prepare for their future roles. He said, "Yes." And we said, "As future leaders?" He waited and then he said, "Where is the word *mother?*"

All my life I have been passionate about being a mother. I feel and have always felt that I could impact the world more by being a good mother and raising a righteous, qualified family than by anything else I could do. I received my degree in English and education at Brigham Young University and then promptly became a teacher—in my own home. In fact, the joke is that our son Matt went through graduation before I did. I am proud to be the mother of five great sons and one wonderful daughter.

And now I am a grandmother. I am still trying to decide whether I like this role. I love the little grandchildren, but I don't like it when their parents take them home. Somehow, it is an adjustment to not have children in our home constantly. On the other hand, there are some pluses. I go grocery shopping alone and, instead of children in the cart, I actually put food. I have intelligent conversations with my husband. Our home is quiet and clean, and I have time to pursue my interests and my passions. The only thing is—those interests and passions all revolve around my family. Really, being a mother defines my life.

When our granddaughter Caroline arrived in the world, our entire extended family gathered to welcome this new little one into our world. As we stood next to the glass and viewed this precious baby asleep in the hospital nursery, we must have made quite a sight. The nurse in the nursery came out and said, "Give

me your camera. The picture from *inside* the nursery, looking out at each of you, is the best picture. I want this little girl to know how many people are here who love her already." Indeed, that is a precious picture, and the nurse's observation was true. We love our granddaughter more than words can express, and we have great expectations for her life. I have felt that same wonder and awe at the birth of each of our children, and now it has returned in the arrival of our grandchildren. Not only do we have great expectations for them, but so does our Father in Heaven.

We can have eternal influence as mothers as we understand the power of our influence on future generations, as we stay focused on the things that matter most, as we make our homes a refuge from the world, as we help our children follow the example of Jesus, and as we draw upon the powers of heaven to help us.

INFLUENCE

We can never measure the extent of our influence. When my daughter-in-law Annie went to her family home to pack its contents after her mother passed away, she was heartbroken. She said how hard it had been. She asked, "How do you pack up a life and put its contents in little boxes and distribute it to whomever?"

My response was, "You don't. You only pack things. Life goes on in the evidence, and the evidence is *you*. It is your life well lived. It is your example. It is you carrying on the things your mother taught you and honoring your heritage and legacy by making honorable and good choices. It is you passing on all that your mother taught you. Her life is not in a box." It is really true—the lives of mothers affect generations.

Belle Spafford, a former general president of the Relief Society and a woman I admire greatly, was asked this question by a friend: "'If someone came to you, Sister Spafford, and had a good but different gift in each hand, and one was power and the other was influence and you had a choice, which gift would you choose?'"

Sister Spafford says she "thought of this seriously for a moment and then . . . said, 'I think I would choose influence.'"

Her friend replied wisely, telling Sister Spafford, "'Influence is a great gift of God to women. . . . Appreciate it and use it aright'" ("Woman in Today's World," 5).

I realized the power of a mother's influence when I visited our oldest son, Matt, who had accepted an internship in New York. When I went to his apartment, I was pleasantly surprised at how neat and tidy it was! In his bathroom I noted that he folded the towels just like ours at home. I also noted that his kitchen was organized exactly like our kitchen at home. He even bought the same brands of food products, and before I even opened the cupboards, I could anticipate what was inside. I had never considered all the things that my son had unconsciously learned from me, but it became graphically clear on that visit.

When my husband and I were newly married, we read a scholarly article by another Dalton—Eugene Dalton—who was a professor at BYU. The article was entitled "Insight and Responsibility." In it he said that studies had verified that whatever the parents discuss in the home is internalized by the

children. Thus, if the parents are critical of a Church leader, even in a casual sense, the children will not only internalize this criticism but they will amplify it. Instead of also being critical of that Church authority, they may amplify that one step further by not attending church at all. That was both shocking and wonderful news, and we used it to our advantage. We always made it a policy to be positive in how we spoke of other people, family members, Church leaders, and even teachers at school, assuming that our children would also amplify positive comments and feelings. And they have!

You might be hearing from the world that you are wasting your time and talent and education by being a mother, but more and more professional women are abandoning the workplace in favor of being full-time mothers. They do not want to turn the nurture and rearing of their children to someone else. Why? Because it is an innate gift of women to nurture. It is in our homes that the true measure of the civilization of our society is evident. As Elder Neal Maxwell taught:

"When the real history of mankind is fully disclosed, will it feature the echoes of gunfire or the shaping sound of lullabies? The great armistices made by military men or the peacemaking of women in homes and in neighborhoods? Will what happened in cradles and kitchens prove to be more controlling than what happened in congresses? When the surf of the centuries has made the great pyramids so much sand, the everlasting family will still be standing, because it is a celestial institution, formed outside telestial time. The women of God know this" ("The Women of God," 10–11).

Barbara Bush, wife of former United States President George H. W. Bush, said to a graduating class at Wellesley College: "Whatever the era . . . whatever the times, one thing will never change: fathers and mothers, if you have children . . . they must come first. Your success as a family . . . our success as a society . . . depends not on what happens at the White House, but on what happens inside your house" (*Barbara Bush: A Memoir*, 540).

Focus

It is our influence more than our power that will shape and change the world. Isn't it amazing that the most important roles are made to look the least important by the world? That is why it is so important to stay focused on the things that matter most.

One young mother asked me if I had written a book about mothering. I told her no! I had been too busy being a mother. She said, "I really want to be a good mother, but it is just so hard and there are so many distractions. I keep being pulled in different directions. I need to know where to focus. I want to be a good mother but I also want to be a person!"

What I heard her saying was that she was not being validated in the world. She felt pulled. Her contribution of mothering was not being recognized for what it was. That makes it harder for us to keep our focus and our priorities straight.

It has been around twenty years since I received a panicked telephone call from a dear friend. I was helping her with the interior design of her new home. She asked me to come as quickly as I could. When I arrived, she took me to the living room. There,

on her brand-new grand piano, was carved a game of tic-tac-toe. Her twins had been left to practice together and instead had busied themselves with the game—on the piano. And they had played it to the end, with the winner carving a line through the three O's in a row. She asked me what to do and we both cried. Then it came to me: "Leave it, Jean," I told her. "In twenty years this will be your most treasured possession."

Twenty years later, I visited Jean and photographed the piano—with those two handsome twins, now young men newly home from serving missions, sitting there. And Jean readily admits that this is the most precious piece of furniture she has in her home, made so because her focus was on her family rather than her possessions.

When "The Family: A Proclamation to the World" was first read in a general Relief Society meeting in 1995, I thought, "That's nice. It's a statement of life as we know it." Little did I realize how timely that document was. It came at a time when lines and roles were being blurred. It came when younger women were hearing very loud voices from the world. It defined some very important things for me and also for my children that aren't being defined by the world at large. The Proclamation clearly teaches that the family is ordained of God and is central to our Creator's plan for the eternal destiny of His children. I am so grateful for this document, which keeps clear the divine design of the family and our roles in it. It is a fundamental teaching piece for our children and grandchildren. The world is not making these clear definitions of the role of the family or the role of mothers and fathers. And yet, almost every social ill can be traced to a lack in these same areas.

MAKING OUR HOMES A REFUGE

In today's gray world, we can and must make our homes a place of refuge. They can be places of light and peace and acceptance. In a publication called *The Family in America,* Bryce Christensen discusses the importance of this. He writes that the number of homeless people on the street "does not begin to reveal the scope of homelessness in America. For since when did the word home signify merely physical shelter, or homelessness merely the lack of such shelter? . . . Home [signifies] not only shelter, but also emotional commitment, security, and belonging. Home has connoted not just a necessary roof and warm radiator, but a place sanctified by the abiding ties of wedlock, parenthood, and family obligation; a place demanding sacrifice and devotion, but promising loving care and warm acceptance" ("HomeLess America," http://www.profam.org/pub/fia/fia_1701.htm).

In my calling as Young Women general president I have had the opportunity to travel to many places in the world. I have visited in the homes of many cultures. Many are very humble. And yet, as I visit, I sometimes find myself wishing that I personally had only *one* chair and *one* small table and *one* frying pan and *one* dress. In these kinds of homes, there are no distractions, and although life is not easy, the family is usually thriving and happy.

Recently I was intrigued by several articles in the newspaper talking about the power of having family dinner together. The research on the effects of a family meal together is quite startling in regard to teenagers. Recent research has affirmed that "the more

children eat dinner with their families, the less likely they are to smoke, drink or use drugs" (in Weaver, "Recipe for drug-free kids").

"The magic that happens at family dinners isn't the food on the table, but the conversations around it," reports a study from the National Center on Addiction and Substance Abuse at Columbia University. "Three in four teens report that they talk to their parents about what's going on in their lives during dinner; and eight in 10 parents agree that by having family dinner they learn more about what's going on in their teens' lives. These conversations are key: Teens who say that they talk to their parents about what's going in on their lives over dinner are less likely to smoke, drink and use marijuana than teens who don't have such talks with their parents."

The study continues: "Teens who have frequent family dinners are almost three times as likely to say they have an excellent relationship with their mother and three times likelier to say they have an excellent relationship with their father; they are also more than twice as likely to report that their parents are very good at listening to them.

"Teens themselves understand the value of family dinners: nearly three-quarters of teens think that eating dinner together with their parents is important. Most teens (60 percent) who have dinner with their parents fewer than five nights a week wish they could eat dinner with their parents more often" ("Importance of Family Dinners VI").

Family traditions also make our homes a refuge from the world. One of our traditions has been that when it is your birthday, you get breakfast in bed. Once I forgot one of our son's birthdays. How terrible! When I went to his room, he was still lying in bed waiting for his breakfast! It was important to him, and I have been delighted to see our children carry this tradition into their own homes.

Traditions can be simple, but they can have a powerful unifying effect. Several years ago, I finally broke down and bought a wheat grinder and a bread mixer. I wanted one of my children's memories to be the smell of freshly baked bread. I think that is because of what my own mother did every Monday.

There are so many loud voices in the world and so many pressures and so much negative feedback. Our children are constantly being told that they are not enough. They are not good enough, or smart enough, or thin enough, or rich enough. When they walk through the doors of our homes, they must feel that they are enough. They must feel peace. Our homes must not be places of additional stress and pressure. They must be havens where each of our children can be valued and loved for just being themselves. As mothers, our role is to love and lead our children. In the words of Sheri Dew, "If we don't show them there is joy in living this way, where else can they possibly expect to see it!" (*No One Can Take Your Place*, 33).

FOLLOWING THE EXAMPLE OF JESUS

Several years ago my husband and I went to the Holy Land. When we arrived in Jerusalem, I was ecstatic. It was a dream come true for me. I had studied and longed to go to the place that the Savior called His home—to walk where He walked, to see what

He saw, and to feel what He felt. As we walked the streets of the city of Jerusalem, I could not get the words of the Primary hymn out of my mind:

Jesus once was a little child,
A little child like me.
And He was pure and meek and mild
As a little child should be.
So, little children,
Let's you and I
Try to be like Him,
Try, try, try.
(*Children's Songbook,* 55)

And each day, that is what we can do—*try!*

As we ponder how to teach and guide our children, it is helpful to understand the process by which Jesus Christ grew spiritually. The process He followed is the same one He asks us to follow. It is a process any of us can incorporate into our lives and into our homes.

Little is recorded about Jesus' youth, but what is recorded is rich with application for us in our lives. Luke tells us that Jesus "increased in wisdom and stature, and in favour with God and man" (Luke 2:52). In other words, He grew intellectually, physically, spiritually, and socially. John tells us that "he received not of the fulness at first, but continued from grace to grace" (Doctrine and Covenants 93:13). So what was the process?

First—He was taught by His mother, Mary, and her husband, Joseph. They had been prepared to be His parents and they had been prepared to raise Him. They had been tutored by an angel—Gabriel—regarding His mission and destiny. They had even been told what His name should be. They had a special knowledge about His identity, and I have no doubt that they taught Him who He was.

We are not so unlike Mary and Joseph. Every mother has a sense of her child's potential when he or she is born. It is innate and sacred. I remember the prayers I offered as my children lay in my arms that I could be capable and worthy enough to help my children fulfill their mortal missions. I prayed then and even now that Steve and I could teach them all the things they would need to know and do. I have little doubt that Mary and Joseph were knowledgeable and highly effective teachers of the Savior in His formative years.

Second, He learned to pray. His parents taught Jesus to pray when He was just a child. I think He learned much through prayer. It was through prayer that He grew close to His Father and learned of His identity and purpose here on the earth. The scriptures don't tell us that, but they do tell us how important prayer was to Him as He grew older. His ministry began with prayer as He went into the wilderness and fasted and prayed for forty days. He often went to the mountains to pray. His disciples even pleaded with Him, "Lord, teach us to pray" (Luke 11:1). His ministry closed in the same way it began—with prayer, this time in the Garden of Gethsemane and on the cross. We too can develop the capacity to pray and to learn through that process.

Third, Jesus was led by the Holy Ghost. He not only prayed but had been taught how to listen and how to qualify for the

guidance of the Holy Ghost. He knew the doctrine of His Father and He learned it through the Holy Ghost's tutoring. He received the Holy Ghost following His baptism, just as our children do. He, however, received a fullness of the Holy Ghost. The Apostle John tells us, "God giveth not the Spirit by measure unto him. The Father loveth the Son, and hath given all things into his hand" (John 3:34–35). In contrast, we receive the Holy Ghost line upon line, here a little and there a little (see 2 Nephi 28:30). He must have been given time by His parents away from the carpenter shop and demands of life and school to "be still" and know God. This would have been important to Him and to His parents. We can do the same for our children. We can keep them and put them in places where they can become acquainted with the Spirit, where they feel its warmth and guidance, where they recognize its promptings.

Fourth, He had a close relationship with His Father. I think that relationship and pattern was established by his earthly father, Joseph, as he worked side by side with his son. It feels to me that as Jesus was daily tutored by His earthly father, Joseph, in informal settings, it was a simple matter to know of His Heavenly Father. I think Jesus knew that His Heavenly Father loved Him because He also knew and experienced His earthly father's love and companionship.

How we love our children will be how they will love theirs. Our relationships with our children are patterns they will remember and pass on to others. They are heavenly patterns.

Fifth, He was familiar with the scriptures. This had to be a major contributor to His knowledge. He was familiar with the scriptures at an early age. Indeed, His relationship to the scriptures was different from that of any human being because he was the Lord God of Israel, Jehovah, who gave those scriptures to the prophets who wrote them. He was found in the temple teaching from the scriptures when He was just twelve years old. He must have been diligent in searching the scriptures for answers and knowledge. When He began His ministry, and Satan tempted him in the desert, He refuted the adversary's attempts with scripture. Scriptures strengthened Him, helped Him resist temptation, and guided Him. On the road to Emmaus, after His crucifixion, Jesus used the scriptures to teach the two disciples the purpose of His mission and His part in the plan of salvation. The two men said, when they finally recognized Him as the Savior, "Did not our heart burn within us, while he talked with us by the way, and while he opened to us the scriptures?" (Luke 24:32).

Jesus was righteous, and His understanding of the scriptures came quickly to Him through study, prayer, and the Holy Ghost. Scriptures were the key element in the Savior's growth from "grace to grace" (Doctrine and Covenants 93:13). Likewise, they can be the key element in our personal spiritual growth and in our children's growth. They can protect and fortify our children. They can change hearts.

CALLING UPON THE POWERS OF HEAVEN

I don't know of any family that doesn't need the help of heaven. Pray with your family. This is one thing you can do to make your home a refuge against the dark world outside. Again,

the Proclamation on the Family states that "successful families are established and maintained on principles of faith and prayer."

Terrorist activities and ongoing armed conflicts underscore the fact that we live in a world of uncertainty and evil. Never has there been a greater need for righteous mothers, mothers who bless their children with a sense of safety, security, and confidence about the future. Mothers who teach their children where to find peace and truth and that the power of prayer is stronger than any other power on the earth.

When I was young, my father became seriously ill. We thought it was just the flu, but as the days progressed, he became more and more ill. It was during that time that I really learned what it means to "pray always" (2 Nephi 32:9). I had a constant prayer in my heart, and I would seek solitary places where I would pour out my soul in prayer to my Heavenly Father to heal my father.

After a few weeks of illness, my father passed away. I was shocked and frightened. What would our family do without our father whom we loved so dearly? How could we go on? I felt that Heavenly Father had not heard or answered my fervent prayers. My faith was challenged. I went to Heavenly Father and asked the question—"Heavenly Father, are you really there?"

I shall never forget our mother gathering us around her the evening of my father's funeral. I was in my teens, and my two brothers were younger. She said that we needed to rely on Heavenly Father now more than ever before because we did not have an earthly father in our home. We kneeled and offered family prayer together. I shall never forget the secure feeling those prayers gave me each day.

Over a period of many months after my father's death, I prayed for help and guidance. I prayed for my family, and I prayed to understand why my father had not been healed. For a time, it seemed to me that the heavens were silent, but as a family we continued to pray for comfort and guidance. I continued to pray also. Then one day, many months later, as I was sitting in a sacrament meeting, my answer came in the form of a scripture. The speaker said: "Trust in the Lord with all thine heart; and lean not unto thine own understanding. In all thy ways acknowledge him, and he shall direct thy paths" (Proverbs 3:5–6). A feeling came over me, and I felt I was the only person in the chapel. That was my answer. Heavenly Father had heard my prayers!

When our circumstances are less than ideal, we as mothers can rely on the power of prayer. We can teach our children that they too can rely on the power of prayer to protect and guide them in today's world.

One mother wanted more than anything else to have a good relationship with her son, but he had taken up with the wrong crowd and had become angry and defiant. She quit her job so that each day she could pick her son up from school and take him directly home, protecting him from the worldly influences. Her son resented that. One night while praying about what to do, she felt impressed that she should love her son and tell him so. But she knew he would not listen to her because they had not had any communication. When they did talk, it was always in anger. Each

time she prayed, the feeling persisted: "Tell your son you love him." But she just couldn't find the right moment.

Then one night she went downstairs to get the laundry. Her son's bedroom was next to the laundry room. She went in and looked at her sleeping son and said quietly, but out loud, "I love you even if you don't know it. Regardless of what happens, I will always love you." She felt good and thought, "There, I finally did it." Even if her son was sleeping and could not hear her, she felt good just saying those words.

Every night thereafter, when she was sure her son was asleep, she would tiptoe into his room and tell him she loved him, sometimes lightly stroking his hair, sometimes kneeling by the bed to gently hold him, taking care not to wake him. Even when he stayed out with his awful friends, she would wait until he had come in and gone to sleep and then go into his room and tell her son that she loved him.

When her son turned fifteen, he went to high school and, in the transition, made some new friends. His attitude slowly got better and his disposition became more positive. He graduated from high school and was called to serve a mission for the Church.

One day, shortly after he returned from a successful mission, some neighbors visited his family's home for advice. They had a wayward daughter and had remembered the difficult times this family had had with their son. The mother told them, "You just have to weather it. Somehow they outgrow it; it is just a phase." But her son interrupted her. "Mom, that's not it! Don't you remember? Every night you would come into my room and say 'I love you' before I went to sleep." His mother's love had been his refuge against a darkening world, a shelter from the storm, a light welcoming him home (see Frandsen, "Refuge," 261–62). Love is the greatest power and will have the most powerful influence.

I believe President Gordon B. Hinckley was absolutely right when he said, "Mothers can do more than any other group to reverse today's sobering social trends" ("Walking in the Light of the Lord," 100). We are mothers whether we have children in our homes or not. We can be mothers to others' children and nurture and warn and protect and love them too. Who knows what our influence might do? If we really want to make a difference, it will happen as we mother our own children and any other children who need us.

I close with several steps that any one of us could take to help the next generation train to run well their own marathon of life:

- Teach them of their divine identity and purpose in the plan of happiness.
- Help them know that it is possible to remain pure in a polluted world.
- Accept and love them wherever they are on the path.
- Rivet their eyes on the words of the latter-day prophets.
- Never underestimate their spiritual capacity or hunger.
- Help them have confidence in personal prayer and receiving answers.
- Help them receive, recognize, and rely on the Holy Ghost.

- Create a climate in which they feel the Spirit in their lives.

- Encourage their questions.

- Help them connect doctrine with their everyday lives.

- Focus on the basics—faith, repentance, baptismal ordinances, the gift of the Holy Ghost, and endurance to the end.

- Teach the blessings of the temple ordinances and eternal families.

- Teach and testify of the Atonement.

Never forget the difference we can make through our influence. As we stay focused on the things that matter most, make our homes refuges from the chaos of the world, follow the example of Jesus, and draw upon the powers of heaven, I believe we can change the world.

Chapter 9

CHEERING THEM ON

Some Words for Those Who Will Follow

Because of my stewardship at this time of my life in my calling as Young Women general president, I want to end this book with a chapter directed to the youth, although I hope the rest of my readers will "listen in" and feel the spirit of what I want to say. Please know that I am talking to you.

To begin with, I want to reacquaint you with your divine identity—who you are and where you are at this time in the Lord's great plan of happiness.

"Even before [you] were born, [you,] with many others, received [your] first lessons in the world of spirits and were prepared to come forth in the due time of the Lord to labor in his vineyard for the salvation of the souls of men" (Doctrine and Covenants 138:56). Alma tells us that you were "called and prepared from the foundation of the world according to the foreknowledge of God, on account of [your] exceeding faith and good works" (Alma 13:3). That "exceeding faith" was in the plan of happiness that was ordained by our Heavenly Father. You had faith in the Savior's ability to make our return to Him possible through His infinite Atonement. Your exceeding good works were manifest as you used your agency to testify to others of the plan and the Savior's role in the plan. You knew the plan was good and you knew the Savior would do what He said He would do—because you *knew* Him!

I hope you know that you belong to the greatest and most powerful group in all the world. You belong to The Church of Jesus Christ of Latter-day Saints, and the future is in your hands. Your combined righteous lives and example have the potential to change the world.

My heart is filled with hope and joy when I see the resolution in your faces and the bright light of the gospel shining in your eyes. When I think of you, I remember the scripture in Alma that says: "And they were among the people of Nephi, and also numbered among the people who were of the church of God. And they were also distinguished for their zeal towards God, and also towards men; for they were perfectly *honest* and upright in all things; and they were *firm* in the faith of Christ, even unto the end" (Alma 27:27; emphasis added). I see in you the shining hope of the future.

I have asked the question many times as I have visited with youth: "Can one virtuous young woman or one righteous young man change the world?" I ask this same question of you: "Do you believe that you have the potential to change the world for good?"

President Thomas S. Monson's life should serve as a reminder that each of you has the potential to have an impact in the world. In fact, I believe that one virtuous young man or young woman with a testimony of the restored gospel of Jesus Christ in his or her heart can change the world. Never before has there been a time of such limitless opportunity to connect with others in the world, to serve, to become educated, and to make a difference. The prophets have said of your day: "And it shall come to pass in the last days, saith God, I will pour out of my Spirit upon all flesh: and your sons and your daughters shall prophesy, and your young men shall see visions" (Acts 2:17).

That prophecy will be fulfilled as you commit to stand on your feet and belong to the chosen generation, setting aside the distractions and worldly influences that surround you. As you decide to do those things that will strengthen your faith in the Savior, and as you live with exactness the Lord's standards found in the *For the Strength of Youth* booklet, you will become a force for good in the world. You will be guided as was Nephi, "not knowing beforehand the things [you] . . . should do" (1 Nephi 4:6). Having faith in the Savior and purifying your lives will enable you to have the constant companionship of the Holy Ghost, and through that power you may accomplish the great things you have been sent to the earth and prepared to do.

Young women, in a world ever growing in moral pollution, tolerance of evil, exploitation of women, and distortion of roles, you must stand guard of yourself, your family, and all those with whom you associate. You must be guardians of virtue.

What is virtue and what is a guardian? As stated in the Young Women Personal Progress booklet (2009), "Virtue is a pattern of thought and behavior based on high moral standards. It includes chastity and [moral] purity." And what is a guardian? A guardian is someone who protects, shields, and defends (see *Webster's New World College Dictionary,* s.v. "guardian"). Thus, as a guardian of virtue, you will protect, shield, and defend moral purity because the power to create mortal life is a sacred and exalted power and must be safeguarded until you are married. Virtue is a requirement to have the companionship and guidance of the Holy Ghost. You will need that guidance in order to successfully navigate the world in which you live.

What can you do to be a guardian of virtue? It starts with believing you can make a difference. It starts with making a commitment. When I was a young woman, I learned that some decisions need to be made only once. I wrote my list of things I would always do and things I would never do in a small tablet. My "always" list included things like obeying the Word of Wisdom, praying daily, paying my tithing, and committing to never miss church. I made those decisions once, and then, in the moment of decision, I knew exactly what to do because I had decided beforehand. When my high school friends said, "Just one drink won't hurt," I laughed and said, "I decided when I was twelve not to do that." Making decisions in advance will help you be guardians of virtue. I hope you will write a list of things you will always do and things you will never do. Then live your list.

Being a guardian of virtue means you will always be modest, not only in your dress but also in your speech, your actions, and your use of social media. Being a guardian of virtue means you will never text words or images to young men that may cause them to lose the Spirit, lose their priesthood power, or lose their virtue. It means that you understand the importance of chastity because you also understand that your body is a temple and that the sacred powers of procreation are not to be tampered with before marriage. You understand that you possess a sacred power

that involves the holy responsibility of bringing other spirits to earth to receive a body in which to house their eternal spirit. This power involves another sacred soul. You are a guardian of something "more precious than rubies" (Proverbs 3:15). Be faithful. Be obedient. Prepare now so that you may qualify to receive all the blessings that await you in the Lord's holy temples.

Despite all the turmoil in the world today, you have a great and promising future. You have been reserved to be on the earth at a time when both the challenges and the opportunities are the greatest they have ever been. No other generation has faced what you are and will face in your lifetime. As I visit with many of you, I am absolutely convinced that you are "come to the kingdom for such a time as this" (Esther 4:14). You are bright. You are good. You have been blessed with the companionship of the Holy Ghost, and because of this gift, you stand out. You are leaders. Thank you for all you are doing and striving to become. I believe that you are the "chosen generation" spoken of by the Apostle Peter (see 1 Peter 2:9.) You have been brought "out of darkness" into the marvelous light of the restored gospel of Jesus Christ. You have been given all the tools that will enable you to make a successful journey—prophets, priesthood, scriptures, the Holy Ghost, family, and leaders. And you have been uniquely positioned at this time and place, distinguished for your faith, your capacity, and your obedience, to successfully fulfill your earthly mission.

DISTINGUISHED FOR YOUR FAITH

Your faith must be firmly centered on Jesus Christ. Having that kind of faith means that you rely on Him, you trust in Him, and, even though you do not understand all things, you know that He does. You know also that He knows you by name and that He will help you accomplish your earthly mission as you turn to Him in prayer.

Enos was a great example of one who went to the Lord in fervent prayer. I believe he wanted to become "more fit for the kingdom" (*Hymns,* no. 131). He had been given a very important calling by his father just prior to his father's death. He knew that he must be true to his father and to that which his father had entrusted to him. He knew that he could not do it alone. So he prayed all day and into the night, and then he heard a voice saying, "Enos, thy sins are forgiven thee, and thou shalt be blessed" (Enos 1:5). When Enos heard these words he asked, "Lord, how is it done?" (v. 7), and the Lord responded: "Because of *thy faith* in Christ, whom thou hast never before heard nor seen" (v. 8; emphasis added). It was his faith that enabled him to receive a remission of his sins. With this pronounced blessing, Enos knew that he could go forward with faith and that he would have the purity and the power to accomplish the task of keeping the sacred record, handed down for generations. Enos then expressed the desires of his heart in prayer and again the Lord answered: "I will grant unto thee according to thy desires, because of *thy faith.* . . . Whatsoever thing ye shall ask *in faith,* believing that ye shall

receive in the name of Christ, ye shall receive it" (Enos 1:12, 15; emphasis added). Enos states simply but powerfully: "And I had faith" (Enos 1:16).

That promise is not only for Enos. It is for you also. And as you do those things that will increase your faith, such as reading daily in the Book of Mormon and praying daily, you too will receive the same blessings promised to Enos.

Did you know that through the power of your faith you can overcome temptation? When Helaman received from his father Alma the same sacred records Enos had kept, he was told that it would be by those small, simple, daily things that great things would be brought to pass. Like Enos, God entrusted Helaman with an important responsibility that would bless him personally and also future generations. Your faithfulness now will bless future generations. In Alma we read: "Now remember, my son, that God has entrusted you with these things, which are sacred . . . that he may show forth his power unto future generations" (Alma 37:14). Always remember that the choices you make and the things you do or do not do are not just about you. They affect future generations—your future family, children, grandchildren, and beyond. Like Helaman, your work is to keep the commandments. You have the capacity and you have the strength and you will be able to "withstand every temptation of the devil, [through your] faith on the Lord Jesus Christ" (Alma 37:33). Armed with the shield of faith, you will be able to quench all the fiery darts of the wicked (see Ephesians 6:16).

All over the world I see faithful youth who keep at the forefront of their minds the importance of faith in the Lord Jesus

Christ. They don't have easy lives. They have very little of material possessions, and yet they are filled with faith and hope for the future. In Africa when I visited with a group of young women, I asked them what challenges they faced as Latter-day Saints. They were silent. Then one young woman in the back of the room stood and said, "Sister Dalton, it is true, we do have many challenges on a daily basis. But, Sister Dalton, we have the restored gospel of Jesus Christ!"

High on the Alto Plano of Bolivia, a young woman wakes each morning at 5:00 A.M. and readies herself to attend seminary. She is the only member of the Church in her family. She has great faith and great determination to grow in the gospel and in her testimony. She washes in a bucket outside the door of her small home, opens a rusty metal gate, and walks out into the darkness so she can go to seminary and walk into the light of the restored gospel of Jesus Christ. I hope each of you, in your busy and scheduled lives, make seminary and Mutual activities a priority. Your spiritual education must not be your last priority, even though it does not appear on a resume or a college application. It appears in your countenance and in your eyes. The confidence you gain by putting the Lord first cannot be underestimated.

DISTINGUISHED FOR YOUR CAPACITY TO PRESS FORWARD

In a talk entitled "Perseverance," President James E. Faust once shared: "When I was your age I used to wonder, 'What will

be my place in this world, and how will I find it?' At that time about my only firm goal was to serve a mission. When my mission call came, I served, and my mission became like the North Star to guide me into the other pursuits of my life. One of the important things I learned was that if I faithfully persevered in my Church callings, the Lord would open up the way and guide me to other opportunities and blessings, even beyond my dreams." He also said, "Perseverance is demonstrated by those who keep going when the going gets tough, who don't give up even when others say, 'It can't be done.'" ("Perseverance," 51).

Several years ago, I had the opportunity to run the Boston Marathon. I had trained hard and felt I was prepared, but at mile twenty there are hills. The locals call the steepest and longest one Heartbreak Hill. When I reached that point, I was physically spent. The hill was long, and because I was a novice, I allowed myself to do something no seasoned runner ever does—I started to think negatively. It grew cold, the wind started to blow, and the rain came in from the east with gale force. I realized what was happening, and so I tried to visualize the finish line. But as I did this, I realized that I was in a big city and there were thousands of people lining the route, and I had not made any arrangements to locate my husband at the end of the marathon. I felt lost and I started to cry.

I was wearing a big red T-shirt with the word *Utah* printed in big white block letters on the front and back. As the spectators saw that I was crying, they would yell: "Keep going, Utah. Don't cry, Utah. You're just about to the finish, Utah!" But I knew I wasn't, and I was lost. Even if I stopped running and dropped out of the race, I would still be lost.

Crossing the Boston Marathon finish line

Do you ever feel like you're running a marathon in your life and the winds are blowing and the sleet is coming at you sideways and you are running up "Heartbreak Hill" and even though there are people lining the route, you are alone? That's how I felt. So I did what every one of you would do—I began to pray right there on that marathon route. I told Heavenly Father that I was alone, and that I was on a hill. I told Him that I was discouraged and afraid and felt lost. I asked for help to find my husband and the strength to finish the race. As I continued to run, these words came into my mind:

> Fear not, I am with you;
> Oh, be not dismayed,
> For I am thy God and will still
> give thee aid.
> I'll strengthen thee, help thee, and
> cause thee to stand,
> Upheld by my righteous,
> omnipotent hand.
> ("How Firm a Foundation," *Hymns,* no. 85)

That sweet answer to my prayer gave me the strength and the courage to continue on until I crossed the finish line. And despite my fears, my husband was right there and all was well.

That day I experienced more than a marathon. I learned some great lessons. First, never wear a big red cotton T-shirt that says *Utah* on it! It soaked up about five pounds of water. But seriously, I learned much more than that. I learned that no matter how well prepared you think you are, there are hills on the course, and sometimes added to the hills will be wind and rain and adverse circumstances that will come upon you, and your own strength to press forward will not be enough. I learned that people cheering for you along the way are absolutely essential. I learned again that day that we are never alone. Our Heavenly Father is only a prayer away, and the Holy Ghost is within whispering distance. The Lord desires to strengthen and to bless us. I also learned that the Atonement is an enabling power. As we turn to the Lord in prayer, He will make our weaknesses our strengths. We can trust in the Lord. You can trust the Lord with all your heart, and your faith will give you power beyond your own.

I learned a great lesson on pressing forward from a group of young women from Alpine, Utah, who decided to focus on the temple by walking from the Draper Utah Temple to the Salt Lake Temple, a total distance of twenty-two miles, just as one of the pioneers, John Rowe Moyle, had done. Brother Moyle was a stonemason who was called by the prophet Brigham Young to work on the Salt Lake Temple. Each week he walked the distance of twenty-two miles from his home to the temple. One of his jobs was to carve the words "Holiness to the Lord" on the east side of the Salt Lake Temple. It was not easy, and he had many obstacles to overcome. At one point, he was kicked in the leg by one of his cows. Because that injury would not heal, he had to have the leg amputated. But that did not stop him from his commitment to the prophet and to working on the temple. He carved a wooden leg, and after many weeks he again walked the twenty-two-mile distance to the temple to do the work he had committed to do (see Uchtdorf, "Lift Where You Stand," 55).

The young women in the Cedar Hills Sixth Ward decided to walk that same distance for an ancestor and also for someone who was their inspiration to remain worthy to enter the temple. They trained each week at Mutual, and, as they walked, they shared what they were learning and feeling about temples.

They began their walk to the temple early in the morning with a prayer. As they started out, I was impressed with their confidence. They had prepared well, and they knew they were prepared. Their eyes were set on their goal.

As these young women continued to walk, there were distractions along the course, but they stayed focused on their goal. Some began to feel blisters forming, and others felt knees starting to protest, but they kept going. For each of you, there are many distractions, hurts, and obstacles along your path to the temple, but you too are determined and keep going. The route these young women took was mapped out by their leaders, who had walked and driven the course and determined the safest and most direct way to go. Again, your course is marked, and you can

be assured that the Savior has not only walked the course but will again walk it with you—every step of the way.

Along this journey to the temple there were fathers, mothers, family members, and priesthood leaders acting as guardians. Their job was to ensure that everyone was safe and protected from danger. They made sure each young woman stayed well hydrated and had enough nourishment to maintain her stamina. There were aid stations provided by their priesthood leaders, with places to rest and to drink water. Your fathers, your mothers, your bishops, and so many others will be your guardians as you walk your path to the temple. They will call out cautions and direct your course, and should you become injured or hurt or get off course, they will help you.

I was impressed that in the final miles of their walk, brothers, other young men, and friends came to support these determined young women and to cheer them on. One brother lifted his sister, who had large blisters on her feet, and carried her on his back the final distance to the temple. As these incredible young women reached their goal, tears were shed as they touched the temple and made a silent commitment to always be worthy to enter there.

My noble, precious friends, as you press forward diligently to obtain the enormous privilege of entering the temple, your course is marked. There will be friends, family members, leaders, and mentors to love you, to cheer for you, and even to lift and carry you over the hard spots, if necessary. But yours are the feet that will walk the path. You must keep your focus and persevere.

DISTINGUISHED FOR YOUR OBEDIENCE

In order feel the power of the Atonement giving you strength to change the world and be a force for good, you will need to be obedient in keeping the commandments. This is one of the reasons you are here on the earth—to see if you will "do all things whatsoever the Lord . . . shall command" (Abraham 3:25). You exercised exceedingly great faith in Him in the premortal existence. You had faith in the Father's plan and in the Savior's ability to be obedient and do what the Father asked Him to do. Your baptismal covenant is a commitment that you always remember the Savior and keep His commandments.

I know that you want to be happy. Maybe you worry about your circumstances. Don't worry. We have the plan of happiness, and keeping the commandments will make you happy! As part of that plan, you were given a body. It is a precious gift whereby you can exercise your agency and put your faith and obedience into action. Your body houses your eternal spirit. Have you ever noticed that nearly all of Satan's attacks are directed at your body? Pornography, immodesty, tattoos, immorality, drug abuse, and addiction are all efforts to take possession of this precious gift. This was a gift he was denied. Care for yourself; be modest and be clean. Do everything you can to be free from anything that would harm your body. Be strictly obedient to the standards in *For the Strength of Youth.* Virtue yields strength, and the blessings of being virtuous are freedom and happiness.

Just like Helaman's stripling warriors, you can be true to all things that are entrusted to you, and as you are true, you will become a mighty army of righteousness.

Now I would like to invite each one of you, the youth of the noble birthright, to do four things daily that will strengthen your faith and help you have the power to obey. This is what I call strict training, and it must be done *daily.* I want you to know that I will not ask you to do anything that I am not personally doing. So we will be doing this together.

First, say your prayers every day—100 percent.

Second, read in the Book of Mormon for five minutes every single day—you can do more if you wish, but the minimum is five minutes—100 percent. Will you do that?

Third—obtain a copy of *For the Strength of Youth* and read it. Then, every day, be strictly obedient to each standard.

Fourth—now for the hard one. I want you to smile every single day—100 percent. Why do I say smile? Because you are blessed. You have the restored gospel of Jesus Christ. Share the joy of living the gospel by smiling. Your friends will wonder what you are up to!

A little hint for remembering the four daily goals is the word *PROS,* standing for *P*ray, *R*ead, *O*bey, and *S*mile. I know—because I am doing them myself—that these four things will strengthen you and enable you to run your race of life successfully!

Whenever we see you, you can give us a sign of thumbs-up or simply say "100 percent" and we'll know that you're with us.

When I was a young woman, my Young Women leaders had each of us choose a symbol that would represent the life we would live and what we would strive to become as daughters of God. We then stitched these symbols onto our bandelos, which were fabric sashes that we wore. I chose the symbol of a white rose because roses become more and more beautiful as they grow and blossom, and I chose the color white for purity.

When I was called to be the Young Women general president, as I was leaving President Monson's office, he reached over to a bouquet of white roses, took one from the vase, and handed it to me. The moment he handed me that beautiful white rose, I knew why. I went back to the time when, as a young woman, I had chosen the white rose as my symbol of purity—my personal banner. How did President Monson know? I took that precious rose home, put it in a beautiful crystal vase, and placed it on a table where I could see it each day. Every day that rose reminded me of the importance of my own personal purity and virtue, and it reminded me of you. Your personal purity will enable you to become a force for good and an influence for righteousness in the world.

It is my prayer that each of you will remember who you are and that you will always be distinguished for your zeal toward God, your faith in Jesus Christ, your capacity to press forward, and your obedience in keeping the commandments and living the standards. I bear you my testimony that He will bless you because

He knows you by name. I testify that He will hear and answer your prayers and strengthen you. He has a great work for you to do. Give it 100 percent, and one day we will be hugging each other and celebrating—victorious—at the finish line!

Hast thou not known? hast thou not heard, that the everlasting God, the Lord, the Creator of the ends of the earth, fainteth not, neither is weary? there is no searching of his understanding.

He giveth power to the faint; and to them that have no might he increaseth strength.

Even the youths shall faint and be weary, and the young men shall utterly fall:

But they that wait upon the Lord shall renew their strength; they shall mount up with wings as eagles; they shall run, and not be weary; and they shall walk, and not faint.

ISAIAH 40:28–31

A Word of Appreciation

First and foremost, I would like to acknowledge my best friend and husband, Steve. He is steady and solid, honest and true. His example and encouragement have helped me move beyond my comfort zones and trained me in consistency and dedication. My family, too, needs to be acknowledged. In my opinion, Matthew, Zachary, Emi, Jesse, Jon, and Chad are champions. They set a fast and steady pace and continue to challenge me to new heights. I am also grateful to each of their spouses—Sheri, Amy, Steve, Annie, Kathy, and Lizzie—for their encouragement and support. I also must acknowledge my mother and father, Emma and Melvin Schwartz, who taught me the gospel without words by the way they lived in our home. My Grandfather Martin was also a great influence in my life. He planted seeds in my heart that are still sprouting and yielding fruit. He simply would not give up against any opposition. I will be eternally grateful to him.

Thanks also to the team at Deseret Book Company: to my friend Sheri Dew for her gentle nudge and encouragement, and to Emily Watts for her brilliant editing, Heather Ward for the innovative design of the book, Tonya Facemyer for the typography, and Jana Erickson for her expertise and help in overseeing all phases of the project.

I also express deep gratitude to my administrative assistant, Kristen Olsen, and my personal secretary, Melissa Lundgreen.

Without all these people, this book could not have happened, and I am deeply indebted to them for their goodness, purity, and virtue.

Finally, I express my eternal gratitude and admiration to the young women of The Church of Jesus Christ of Latter-day Saints. They are remarkable!

SOURCES CITED

Ballard, M. Russell. "Purity Precedes Power." *Ensign,* November 1990, 35–38.

Bednar, David A. "Honorably Hold a Name and Standing." *Ensign,* May 2009, 97–100.

Benson, Ezra Taft. "In His Steps." *Speeches of the Year, 1979.* Provo, UT: Brigham Young University Press, 1980.

———. "The Law of Chastity." *New Era,* January 1988, 4–7.

Bush, Barbara. *Barbara Bush: A Memoir.* New York: Scribner, 1994.

Children's Songbook. Salt Lake City: The Church of Jesus Christ of Latter-day Saints, 1989.

Christensen, Bryce. "HomeLess America: What the Disappearance of the American Homemaker Really Means." *The Family in America.* Online Edition: http://www.profam.org/pub/fia/fia_1701.htm. Last accessed 25 May 2011.

Cracroft, Richard H. and Neal E. Lambert. *A Believing People: Literature of the Latter-day Saints.* Provo: Brigham Young University Press, 1974.

Dew, Sheri. *No One Can Take Your Place.* Salt Lake City: Deseret Book, 2004.

Eyring, Henry B. *Because He First Loved Us.* Salt Lake City: Deseret Book, 2002.

———. "A Child and a Disciple." *Ensign,* May 2003, 29–32.

———. *To Draw Closer to God.* Salt Lake City: Deseret Book, 1997.

"Family: A Proclamation to the World, The." *Ensign,* November 1995, 102.

Faust, James E. "Five Loaves and Two Fishes." *Ensign,* May 1994, 4–7.

———. "Perseverance." *Ensign,* May 2005, 51–53.

For the Strength of Youth: Fulfilling Our Duty to God. Salt Lake City: Intellectual Reserve, 2001.

Frandsen, Shauna U. "Refuge." *May Christ Lift Thee Up: Selections from the 1998 Women's Conference Sponsored by Brigham Young University and the Relief Society.* Salt Lake City: Deseret Book, 1999.

Gates, Susa Young. *History of the Young Ladies' Mutual Improvement Association of the Church of Jesus Christ of Latter-day Saints.* Salt Lake City: Deseret News, 1911.

Hinckley, Gordon B. "An Ensign to the Nations, a Light to the World." *Ensign,* November 2003, 82–85.

———. "Our Responsibility to Our Young Women." *Ensign,* September 1988, 8–11.

———. "Standing Strong and Immovable." Worldwide Leadership Training Meeting, 10 January 2004, Salt Lake City: The Church of Jesus Christ of Latter-day Saints, 2004.

———. "Stay on the High Road." *Ensign,* May 2004, 112–15.

———. "Walking in the Light of the Lord." *Ensign,* November 1998, 97–100.

Holland, Jeffrey R. "What I Wish Every Member Knew—and Every Longtime Member Remembered." *Ensign,* October 2006, 10–16.

Hymns of The Church of Jesus Christ of Latter-day Saints. Salt Lake City: The Church of Jesus Christ of Latter-day Saints, 1995.

"The Importance of Family Dinners VI." The National Center on Addiction and Substance Abuse at Columbia University, September 2010. Downloaded June 29, 2011, from http://www.casacolumbia .org/templates/Publications_Reports.aspx#r81.

Kimball, Spencer W. *Faith Precedes the Miracle.* Salt Lake City: Deseret Book, 1972.

———. "On My Honor." *Ensign,* April 1979, 2–5.

Lukas, John R. *Blood, Toil, Tears, and Sweat: The Dire Warning.* New York: Basic Books, 2008.

Madsen, Susan Arrington. *I Walked to Zion: True Stories of Young Pioneers on the Mormon Trail.* Salt Lake City: Deseret Book, 1994.

Maxwell, Neal A. "The Women of God." *Ensign,* May 1978, 10–11.

Monson, Thomas S. "Examples of Righteousness." *Ensign,* May 2008, 65–68.

Morris, Edmund. *Colonel Roosevelt.* New York: Random House, 2010.

Nelson, Russell M. *Perfection Pending, and Other Favorite Discourses.* Salt Lake City: Deseret Book, 1998.

———. "Personal Preparation for Temple Blessings." *Ensign,* May 2001, 32–35.

Newell, Lloyd D. "Lest We Forget." Music and the Spoken Word broadcast, April 2, 2006.

Preach My Gospel: A Guide to Missionary Service. Salt Lake City: Intellectual Reserve, 2004.

Ruskin, John. *The Seven Lamps of Architecture.* London: Smith, Elder, and Co., 1849.

Sandrock, Michael. *Running with Legends: Training and Racing Insights from 21 Great Runners.* Champaign, IL: Human Kinetics, 1996.

Smith, Joseph F. *Gospel Doctrine: Selections from the Sermons and Writings of Joseph F. Smith.* Edited by John A. Widtsoe. Salt Lake City: Deseret Book, 1919.

Smith, Joseph, Jr. *History of the Church of Jesus Christ of Latter-day Saints.* 7 vols. 2nd ed. rev. Edited by B. H. Roberts. Salt Lake City: The Church of Jesus Christ of Latter-day Saints, 1932–1951.

———. *Lectures on Faith: Delivered to the School of Prophets in Kirtland, Ohio, 1834–1835.* Salt Lake City: Deseret Book, 1985.

Spafford, Belle S. "Woman in Today's World." *BYU Speeches of the Year,* March 3, 1970.

Stevenson, Ford. "Church marks 150 years in Scandinavia." *Church News,* July 15, 2000.

Tanner, John S. "To Clothe a Temple." *Ensign,* August 1992, 44–47.

Sources Cited

Tuttle, A. Theodore. "Your Mission Preparation." *Ensign,* November 1974, 71–72.

Uchtdorf, Dieter F. "Lift Where You Stand." *Ensign,* November 2008, 53–56.

Weaver, Sarah Jane. "Recipe for drug-free kids: Family Dinner." *Church News,* September 8, 2007.

Webster's New World College Dictionary. Fourth Edition. Cleveland, OH: Wiley Publishing, Inc., 2008.

Westfall, Richard S. *Never at Rest: A Biography of Isaac Newton.* New York: Cambridge University Press, 1980.

Young, Brigham. *Discourses of Brigham Young.* Edited by John A. Widtsoe. Salt Lake City: Deseret Book, 1954.

———. *Journal of Discourses.* 26 vols. London: Latter-day Saint Book Depot, 1854–1886.

INDEX

D

E

F

G

H